THE SECRETS OF THE NOTEBOOK

EVE HAAS

LARGE PRINT

Oxford

First published in Great Britain 2009
by
HarperTrue
an imprint of HarperCollins*Publishers*

Published in Large Print 2010 by ISIS Publishing Ltd.,
7 Centremead, Osney Mead, Oxford OX2 0ES
by arrangement with
HarperCollins*Publishers*

British Library Cataloguing in Publication Data
Haas, Eve.
    The secrets of the notebook.
    1. Haas, Eve - - Family.
    2. Haas family.
    3. Prussia (Germany) - - History - - 19th century - -
    Biography.
    4. Germany - - History - - 20th century - -
    Biography.
    5. Large type books.
    I. Title
    943'.07'0922–dc22

ISBN 978-0-7531-9544-4 (hb)
ISBN 978-0-7531-9545-1 (pb)

Printed and bound in Great Britain by
T. J. International Ltd., Padstow, Cornwall

*I dedicate this book to the memory of
Emilie, Charlotte and Anna*

With special thanks to Andrew Crofts and Timothy Haas for their contribution in the writing of this book.

I owe so much to my dearest parents, Hans and Grete, and to my Uncle Freddy and Alice his wife.

My beloved husband Ken was my rock, my three sons, Anthony, Timothy and David my inspiration. Without them my journey could never have taken place.

ANNA JARETZKI

Born Berlin — March 7th, 1864
Died Theresienstadt — August 12th, 1942

"Deeply loved and
never forgotten"

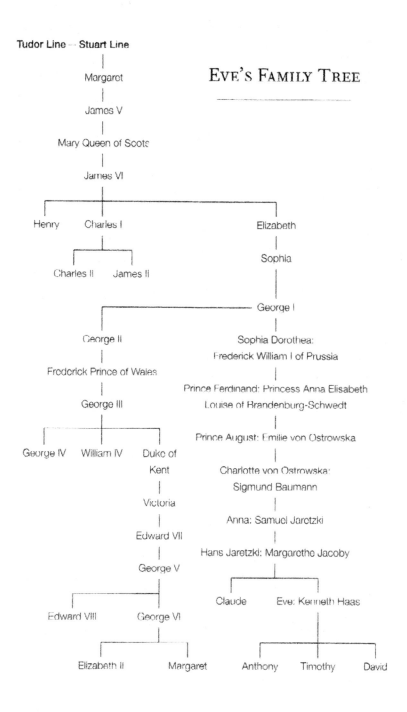

Tudor Line — Stuart Line

EVE'S FAMILY TREE

Margaret

James V

Mary Queen of Scots

James VI

Henry   Charles I   Elizabeth

                                                Sophia

Charles II   James II

                                    George I

    George II   Sophia Dorothea:
                           Frederick William I of Prussia

Frederick Prince of Wales   Prince Ferdinand: Princess Anna Elisabeth
                             Louise of Brandenburg-Schwedt

    George III   Prince August: Emilie von Ostrowska

George IV   William IV   Duke of   Charlotte von Ostrowska:
                         Kent   Sigmund Baumann

                         Victoria   Anna: Samuel Jaretzki

                      Edward VII   Hans Jaretzki: Margarethe Jacoby

                       George V

Edward VIII   George VI   Claude   Eve: Kenneth Haas

Elizabeth II   Margaret   Anthony   Timothy   David

PROLOGUE

The First Glimpse

I saw the notebook for the first time in London in 1940 and was instantly enchanted by the mystery of the story surrounding it. It was wartime and we were in our flat in Hampstead where we had been living ever since we had escaped from Europe in 1934. All through the previous night we had suffered a terrifying air raid, which at dawn had left the three of us feeling shaken.

My father had brought the book to the breakfast table, never having mentioned its existence to me before. It was still in its envelope, tied with a green ribbon. He must have decided that now I had passed my sixteenth birthday it was time for me to be given some knowledge about the family secret. Perhaps he had waited before explaining the little book's history to me until he thought I was old enough to be trusted not to tell anyone else. Or maybe the closeness of the bombs the previous night had reminded him of his own mortality and he didn't want to risk the secret dying with him. I never knew what caused him to choose that morning to fetch it from wherever he had been hiding it since we'd arrived in London, and to take it from its envelope in front of me.

"What's that?" I asked as he sat down with us.

"Oh, it's nothing," he said, trying to underplay its importance as my mother poured the coffee. "Just a diary."

"I didn't know you kept a diary." I was surprised. In my youthful ignorance I had thought I knew everything about my beloved father.

"Well," he looked uncomfortable for a second, as though he had been caught out not telling the whole truth. Was he having second thoughts about telling me, now that he was sitting beneath my mother's firm and slightly disapproving gaze? "I don't keep a diary," he said with a smile.

"It's just an old family memento," Mother said brusquely, clearly coming to his rescue in some way. I don't know if he had consulted her about telling me that day, or whether he had reached the decision alone, but they exchanged a look that I couldn't understand and then seemed to come to a decision simultaneously to go ahead with the revelation. My father passed the book to me.

"Be careful, Eve," he said, as if I were a small clumsy child who might drop and break it. "It's very old."

It was heavy for something so small and as I cradled it in my hands I saw there was a grand family crest of some sort embossed on the silver gilt cover. It felt solid and substantial as I gently ran my thumb over it. I opened the first page and read out loud the elegantly written inscription inside. It was in German.

"*The beautiful owner of this book is dearer to me than my life — August your protector.*"

I looked up enquiringly but neither of them said anything, both concentrating on their breakfast.

"Who is this August?" I asked.

They exchanged another nervous glance and then my father seemed to decide to take the plunge.

"He was royal," he said. "A Prussian prince. He was your great, great grandfather, Eve."

"Anna's grandfather was a royal prince?" I said after considering the thought for a few moments. I tried to imagine my sweet, arthritis-ridden old grandmother being that closely related to royalty and failed. *Princess Anna* — it seemed too fantastical to be true.

"He married Emilie Gottschalk, the daughter of a Jewish tailor, and . . ." my father seemed to be hesitating; was he wishing he had never started the conversation, eager to squash my enthusiastic curiosity? Was it all too embarrassing to talk about?

"We know very little, and it is only word of mouth," he carried on with conviction, then seemed to want to change the subject as quickly as possible, as if I had now been told all I needed to know and there was no point in going any further. "Except that this little pocket-book is all there is . . ."

"Why is this all there is?" I stroked the little book again. I wasn't going to leave it at that. What sixteen-year-old girl would be willing to dismiss the idea that she might be descended from a prince without coming up with a thousand new questions. "What about Anna's mother? What was her name?"

"Charlotte," my father said, avoiding my eyes and

those of my mother as he continued to eat his breakfast. "She was Prince August's daughter."

"Well," I said, feeling slightly frustrated by how evasive they were both being. "There must be records of her life —"

"Eve," my father put up his hand to stop me in my tracks. "My mother gave me —"

He stopped speaking for a moment, as if mustering enough strength to keep his emotions under control in front of me and I immediately felt guilty for having forced him to talk about my grandmother, Anna, like that. Anna was sending us letters intermittently via the Red Cross, which was in itself very worrying, although she professed to be alright, I knew he was partly hoping that if she did get arrested then she wouldn't linger and would leave this earth before her suffering became too great, while the other half struggled with the idea that he might never see her again, would never be able to say goodbye and might never know the truth of what had happened to her in her final days. My own deep-rooted fears for her safety were distressing for me too, as the truth of the desperate situation for all Jews who remained in German-occupied Prague had begun to dawn on all of us.

We weren't alone in our worries; many Jewish families living in England had had to leave relatives behind for one reason or another when they fled from the murderous hatred that Hitler was spreading throughout mainland Europe. In fact my family was more fortunate than many because my parents were already well travelled, with many friends in other countries. But Anna had been too old and too slowed by her arthritis to be able to come with my Uncle Freddy, my father's brother, and his family when they escaped for the last time from Prague to join us in England in 1938. Both Uncle Freddy and my father had had to put the welfare of their wives and children before that of their elderly mother, especially as she was insistent that she wanted to stay. They had done the right thing, but that didn't mean my father wasn't racked with a painful guilt as a result, tortured by not knowing what had happened or what could be happening in Prague at the very moment that we were sitting round the breakfast table in England. I went back to studying the precious little book in silence for a few moments.

"This little book is all we have," my father said after a few minutes. "It has been handed down through the generations. It is the only proof we have that Emilie and the Prince had a life together and that that is where we came from. When I am no more, this book will be yours to keep and to pass on to the next generation. But you mustn't do anything about it. Remember Eve, there is nothing more to find out. Nothing else has been written, nothing else exists, so don't go looking for it. All we know is what we have learned by word of mouth. Apart from a little portrait of Charlotte's mother, Emilie, which your Uncle Freddy has, this book is all that exists from that time. I wanted you to know that you have blue blood flowing in your veins, that is all. Just be content with that."

In all my innocence I couldn't immediately accept

what he was saying, but I knew enough not to press him any more and I was privileged to think that I had been chosen to be the keeper of such a precious and mysterious heirloom, to be the one to pass the secrets on to the next generation of our family. I adored my father above anything else, but he was sensitive, and a man whose word I respected. If he didn't want me to go looking for any more information about our family's past then I would not question his wishes any further. My father passed the pocket-book to my mother, who promptly put it back into the old yellowing envelope it had come from and slipped the green ribbon over it. Then she left the room. We met again a few minutes later in the kitchen where I was washing up the breakfast things.

Caressing my hair, Mother quietly whispered in my ear, "The King wouldn't allow it, but August went against his wishes and married Emilie anyway."

The events of my childhood in Berlin had taught me just how dangerous it could be to be related to the wrong people or to anger those who held the power of life and death in their hands. To be considered to have the wrong blood flowing in your veins could mean instant arrest and who knew what fate after that. No Jewish family living in Europe during those times wanted to draw attention to themselves in any way at all. The secret to survival was to be as discreet and inoffensive as possible. Going around claiming to be directly descended from one of the wealthiest and most powerful royal families in all history, as I later found out they were, was likely to annoy more people than it would enchant or intrigue, but I still ached to find out more about what sounded like a real-life fairy tale.

My father must have chosen me to give the book to because he knew that I would be captivated by the romance of the story and believed that I would pass the story on to any children I might have, just as he was passing it on to me. He must have believed that the precious book would be in safe and loving hands with me and I still feel touched and honoured to have been chosen to carry the secret on for the next generation. Sitting at the breakfast table that day, however, I had no idea just what an extraordinary journey that little keepsake would eventually take me on, a journey back in time, across closed and dangerous borders to uncover secrets that had been carefully hidden and closely guarded for over a century.

CHAPTER
ONE

Goodbye Berlin – Hello Hampstead

Most of the early years of my life were spent in the political turmoil of Berlin. I was born on my father's birthday, 26 June 1924. My mother went into labour in a state of shock, having been informed by her sister, Fridl, that the Berlin evening paper had announced that my father had been fatally injured that day in a car accident.

In fact my father was not dead, but instead was fighting for his life in a convent in the middle of nowhere. He had been travelling on business from our home in Breslau, which was then in Germany but is now in Poland, when his car was forced off the road by a heavily laden haywain steered by a woman in a red headscarf. Startled by the unexpected sound of an engine the carthorse had reared up. My father loved driving his new Buik 24–54, so he was at the wheel despite the fact that he had his chauffeur with him. He swerved to avoid the flailing hooves and rolled off the road into a ditch, ending up on its side. The chauffeur was thrown clear but my father was trapped inside with a fractured skull and a broken arm and leg.

Clambering to his feet, the chauffeur waved down the next car to pass by, but the driver refused to take "a dying man". The next vehicle to pass was a lorry loaded with bricks and the driver agreed to take my unconscious father to a nearby convent in the hope that the nuns could save him. Having no option the chauffeur accepted the offer and the nuns took him in, in the true Christian spirit. Somehow the news reached the ears of a journalist in Berlin who decided to print the piece as news without further verification.

Father stayed under the tender care of the nuns for five days before he was finally judged strong enough to be transferred to Breslau Hospital, where my mother and I were still patients after my apparently difficult and traumatic arrival.

Things would have been so different if he had died that night on the road, or later in the peace of the convent. If he had passed away that night his mother, Anna, would never have been able to give him the pocket-book, which would later come to me. It would instead have gone to my Uncle Freddy for safekeeping, with our family's mysterious past remaining a secret.

After my dramatic entry into the world, my first few years were stable and pleasant. As a small child I lived in central Berlin with my family all around me. We lived close to my grandparents and to my Uncle Freddy and his family. Freddy and my father were very close, and looked similar too, although Freddy was heavier set and taller than his brother.

My parents, Hans and Margarethe Jaretzki, had married in 1917 after my father was invalided back from the Russian Front during the First World War. My paternal grandfather, Samuel Jaretzki, was a tough, disciplined man, a highly respected stockbroker who was the longest serving member of the Berlin Stock Exchange and didn't want my father to marry my mother, although I have no idea why not. My father however, as quietly determined as ever, simply packed his bags and left home. His mother, Anna, went searching for him and eventually tracked him down in a small hotel. Using all her quiet charm she persuaded her son to come home and she persuaded his father to relent. As a result of her efforts to broker a peace between father and son, my parents' marriage took place.

Hans was an architect, one of a dynasty of Jaretzki architects. Eight of them had practised in Berlin; the last remaining, Frank Jarrett at 98, lives happily in California, where his son, Norman, carries on the family tradition. Some of their buildings remain today, despite nearly eighty per cent of Berlin having been destroyed, first by allied bombs and later by the Russian tanks as they invaded, forcing Hitler's final line of defence to capitulate and surrender. Earlier in 1917 during World War I Hans was injured and invalided away from the frontline when the German Army ordered him in his capacity as an architect and engineer to build munitions factories on the Polish border, and so my parents moved to East Prussia.

My father was a gentle man, softly spoken and thoughtful, different to my mother and always keen to avoid personal conflict or confrontation. My mother was dark-haired, petite and attractive and my father was slightly built and fair.

Two years after they were married they had my brother, Claude, who took after my mother in many ways. I was born five years later and I was much more like Father. Claude grew to be quite tall and handsome and because of their similar personalities he got on very well with our mother. But Grandmother Anna made no secret of the fact that she adored me, and I adored her in return. She indulged me at every opportunity she was given and took a keen interest in my schooling and progress. She used to buy me some special little chocolate figures and I remember at one time I had a very strict governess called Fraulein Mueller who snatched the treasured figures away from me because I wouldn't eat my dinner, and she never returned them. I still regret losing them to this day.

They were happy times for the whole family and I still remember scenes from those days as vividly as if they were yesterday; playing with my friend Lottie Schulz, walking an old lady's dog for her, wrapping up pfennig coins in newspaper, then throwing them to the organ grinder and his performing monkey from our first floor balcony. The man doffed his hat as the monkey picked them up before waving their goodbyes. We lived very comfortably and my mother had the help of both a maid and live-in nanny. I had no inkling at that stage of what terrible times lay ahead.

Anti-Semitism had been endemic in those parts of Europe for centuries, but as a child I was blissfully unaware of that fact, shielded as I was by my loving family, and to begin with I was not aware that the hatred of the Jews was becoming deeper and darker with every passing year. Eventually, however, the truth was inescapable. We stayed in Germany until the spring of 1934, long enough for me to learn the shocking lesson that we were not welcome there, although at the age of nine I was finding it hard to come to terms with why that might be.

I remember Hitler coming to power and wearing my "*Ja for Hitler*" sticker with the same enthusiasm as all the other children I knew. The Brownshirts, a Para-military wing of the Nazi party renowned for its violent methods, were often outside the school after that, menacingly checking that we were displaying our stickers prominently. I was nine years old when I huddled beside the wireless listening to Hitler's victory speech, unnerved by the sombre mood of the adults all around me and finding it hard to really understand why their fears were so great. We could hear the euphoria of the crowds on the streets outside but inside everyone's spirits were brought low with feelings of dread because they had already started to hear rumours and stories about what was happening to Jews in other parts of the country.

At eight o'clock one morning at school we were all assembled as usual in the classroom when we heard an unusual noise. It sounded like the clumping of approaching boots. The door opened and we saw that our teacher had been transformed overnight. The small and usually sober-suited Herr Kähne looked taller and prouder than usual in jackboots and a brown Nazi uniform emblazoned with a swastika armband.

"From now on," he announced loudly, "we no longer pray to God. We pray to Adolf Hitler."

That day as I walked home I noticed that the grocer and baker's shops that we used nearly every day to buy our supplies had been boarded up and the word "JUDE" had been daubed across the boards in large, angry letters. It was an ugly, threatening sight and my disquiet grew when I found my mother was crying as I reached her at the street corner.

"Terrible things are happening," she said, hurrying me back home without elaborating.

Now of course I know that the first pogrom against the Jews had already started as Hitler fed the wave of euphoria that was sweeping through the hearts and minds of young Germans everywhere, but at that moment I was still too young to know about any of that. It was hard for me to understand why everyone else in Germany seemed to be so excited by what was happening when my family and their friends were all so sad and fearful.

Back at school in the following weeks there was always a squabble for one of us to have the honour of carrying the huge Nazi flag at the head of the class on our weekly walks through the "Grunewald", the local wood across the road. One day I insisted it was my turn and pushed eagerly to the front of the class with my hand up. Herr Kähne seemed reluctant but eventually handed it to me, still not quite brainwashed enough to blame a child in his care for belonging to the wrong religion. I had no idea of the significance of my actions as I proudly marched away holding the swastika standard of my class, wanting to belong and to be part of the excitement.

The first time I heard the voices of the Hitler Youth singing the Nazi anthem to the drumbeat of their jackboots they were marching through the city, thousands of them in a sea of brown uniforms. I was out in the street with my friend Lottie. We ran to the front of the crowd to watch and wave, smiling at them happily as they passed. Women were pouring out of their front doors, feting and kissing the boy soldiers and filling their water bottles for them. Seeing this show of military might seemed to fill the hearts and minds of all the onlookers with excitement and anticipation and I found myself infected along with everyone else, completely ignorant of what it was I was cheering for.

But every day things kept happening that puzzled me. Lottie's brother, Hermann, for instance, was so influenced by all the propaganda that he reported his father to the local Hitler Youth Group Leader, denouncing him for speaking against Hitler at home. His father duly received a visit from a Gestapo officer, which effectively silenced him on that subject from then on. Hermann was not unusual in believing that this was the right way to behave, that loyalty to the Führer was far and away more important than loyalty to your own family. I couldn't imagine any circumstances where I would ever dream for even a moment of getting any member of my family into trouble with the authorities, least of all my beloved father.

"The man is insane," my father would insist over and over again whenever the name of Adolf Hitler came up. "I will not live in a country led by a murderer."

My mother accepted that Father was right and that it would soon be too dangerous to be living in Germany, but before we could move they needed to establish where we could go that would be safe. It was through Sir Eric Phipps, the British Ambassador, whose residence he had designed and built in the Berlin suburb of Wannsee, that my father was able to seek the help that he needed from Frank Foley, the British Passport Control Officer stationed in Berlin. Foley, it was recently revealed, was working under cover as Britain's Chief Spymaster in Europe, saving more than 10,000 Jews from certain death by flouting both British and German laws.

My father left first to search for a country that would accept us if we were to flee from Germany. When my mother heard that he had reached England she joined him, having given up our home and left me to stay with her sister, Aunt Fridl, and Claude with friends in Silesia.

They were hoping that we would be able to move to Hampstead in North London. None of my family were practising Jews and my father did not go to synagogue, although he did eventually design one of the biggest ones, situated in Edgware, North London. My father was a well-known Bauhaus architect and a leading light of the modernist Bauhaus design movement, which had started in Germany after the First World War (even though so much of Berlin was destroyed quite a few of his buildings have survived and are now officially protected by preservation orders). His reputation was not going to be enough to protect him against the rising tide of hatred. While my father was away the situation was rapidly deteriorating. In November 1933 the Nazis threw him out of the German Architectural Association (BDA). By this time Reg Calendar, one of Frank Foley's close aides, had arranged for my father to receive a permanent working visa in England, without which he would have been deported back to Germany like so many others. Reg and my father became friends and I remember him visiting our flat in Hampstead with his family. So it was that by early 1934 my parents were making the necessary arrangements for our arrival in England as a family.

I was nine years old and devastated by their departure, and by the thought of having to leave the home I loved. Above all, I missed my father terribly while he was away and was constantly writing him notes on any bits of paper I could find. I was so distraught about all the changes that were going on in my life that I was hardly eating and I was losing weight at an alarming rate. I was terrified that I would never see my father again. My brother was also a long way away, staying with our parents' friends in Silesia and I felt very lost and lonely.

Anti-Semitism was becoming more open and violent every day, even in the little school where I had always been so happy. One day I was singled out and cornered by a group of boys who ripped my glasses off and beat me for no other reason than that I was Jewish and they had learned that they must hate me and that there would be no repercussions for any harm that they might decide to do to me.

Lottie's mother sent some honey cakes to the house for me one day, but my aunt's cook confiscated them before I could take even one bite, fearing that they might have been laced with poison. All Jews were becoming paranoid, but with good reason. We could not be sure who our friends were any more, or who had had their heads turned or who would decide to denounce us in order to save their own skins.

Uniformed Nazis arrived at my aunt's flat, barging their way into the kitchen one lunchtime on "*eintopf tag*" (one pot day), when we had all been told we were only allowed one simple stew — and we had to pay the price of the big meal that we had apparently saved to the country's war chest. They would come checking regularly that our family meal was being confined to one pot as instructed and then demand a considerable sum of money which they said we would have saved with this action — all for "The Führer's Charity". They could take whatever they wanted from us and there was nothing we could do. There was no one we could turn to for justice or protection.

In Spring 1934 my mother appeared back in Berlin announcing that everything was arranged and that she was going to be taking me and my brother Claude to England with her to join our father. I was traumatised at the thought of my life in Berlin coming to such an abrupt end, but excited at the same time to think I would be seeing my darling father again, and relieved to think we would be going somewhere safe and far away from the threatening Brownshirts. The hardest part was being separated from my best friend Lottie, but during a tearful farewell we both swore we would keep on writing to one another forever.

The journey across to England was frightening and overwhelming. There were soldiers and police everywhere and we expected to be stopped and arrested every time anyone looked at us, as we headed to Holland and the port of Hook Van Holland, where we would board our boat. When we finally reached the grey, misty English Channel sea-sickness had consumed me, as the weather was stormy and the boat rolled and tossed violently on the giant waves. As we queued up to leave the train at Liverpool Street a surge of sickness hit me again, partly due also to my mother's insistence that I should start living like a little English girl and breakfast on kippers on the way over. The last thing your stomach wants in a situation like that is an unfamiliar and aromatic smoked fish.

My father was waiting for us anxiously on the station platform and I fell into his arms as he gathered me up in a giant hug. Being with him made me feel like all my troubles were over, and that I would be able to bear being parted from Berlin and Lottie after all. With him there to guide us, the bustle of the station and the foreign voices all around didn't seem so overwhelming. My father strode to the taxi rank and instructed the cabbie to take us to a boarding house in Fairfax Road,

Hampstead, where my parents had been staying during the previous months. The taxi was open-sided and driven by a red-faced man in a flat cap. It seemed like a very British experience and I was grateful for the flow of fresh air to blow away the last lingering flavours of breakfast, despite the biting cold.

When we reached the house I was surprised to find that it was filled with German doctors who worked at the German hospital in London. I was put straight into a big Victorian bedstead with sheets and blankets, another new experience for a child used to an eiderdown and a feather bed, but a great deal more pleasant than the kipper experience. There was an open fireplace in the room and from the chimney I could hear the contented sound of pigeons softly cooing on the roof as I began to slip into an exhausted sleep. It was a sound I had never heard before. I felt so safe in the knowledge that I had been reunited with my father.

The next morning at breakfast we shared our table with a tortoise, which was happily munching away at some lettuce leaves while its owner, an English lady, sipped her coffee like it was the most normal thing in the world.

"The English are great animal lovers," my father explained when he saw my astonished and delighted face.

The next problem was finding a school that could accommodate a child who couldn't speak a word of English, but eventually Kingsley School in Belsize Park, near Hampstead, agreed to accept me. Although it was a relief to be away from the brown uniforms and jackboots, I felt very homesick for my life in Berlin and for Lottie who had shared so much of my life until then, but I didn't complain. I knew that we had had no option, and I would never have questioned my parents' decisions anyway; children didn't do that sort of thing in those days.

Being thrown in the deep end I picked up the English language surprisingly quickly and felt a warm glow of pride when a teacher said in front of the whole class that if she didn't know it was me, she would have thought it was a little English girl reading her essay out loud. As my confidence grew I became a little bit cheeky and was banned from German classes for laughing at the red-haired Miss Jones's German accent. Never allowed to attend her class again I was sent to study Latin instead.

Lottie kept writing to me just as she promised she would, keeping the memories of Berlin alive, telling me how much she missed me and filling me in on everything I was missing. The moment her letters arrived I would rip them open and devour every word, feeling a mixture of excitement at her news and sadness at the reminder of everything I had left behind back home. Some of it was puzzling. She told me, for instance, that her "best hour at school" was on Saturdays when she learned "all about Hitler". Another letter told of her "joy" at having "danced for Hitler". It was 1936 and the occasion was the Olympic Games. I showed the letters to my father in the hope that he would explain why Lottie wasn't as frightened of Hitler as we had been. His face became grave as he read.

Alarmed by her tone, he forbade me from writing to her any more. It didn't occur to me to disobey any direct order he gave me, but it made me deeply miserable as Lottie's letters kept coming, each one expressing greater degrees of puzzlement and hurt at my sudden and unexplained silence. My father's decision, however, would eventually prove to be more than wise.

Meanwhile my grandmother, Anna, was living in Czechoslovakia with her other son, my father's brother Uncle Freddy. He had left Berlin back in 1923, during the Great Depression after World War I, and before Hitler's reign of terror was beginning to take hold. Uncle Freddy had been offered a new job in Brno, Czechoslovakia, working for Himmelreich & Zwicker, a large textile manufacturer, as their export director. By 1933 he had joined Victoria Assurance in Reichenberg as Managing Director. My grandfather, Samuel, died suddenly around that time, at the age of 72, from an undiagnosed twisted bowel, leaving Granny Anna a widow at 68. Influenced by my father's plans to leave, she too must have decided that Berlin was becoming too dangerous because she went to live with Freddy and his family in Reichenberg, which was near Prague. It was while she was there that my brother Claude, who was thirteen years old by then, and I went to visit her for the last time. I spent many hours with her in her room during the two or three weeks we were there. We talked about the family and the future, and she would read me poetry. I had an autograph book, which I asked her to sign. She took it from me with a smile and sat down to write:

When once you are a grandmamma, and sit in the rocking chair with Grandpapa and dream of your joyful childhood days, remember your Oma Annchen.

I can still clearly remember saying goodbye to her after that visit on Prague Railway Station. I wanted to stay wrapped in her loving arms forever but eventually Claude had to take me by the hand and lead me to the departing train, otherwise it would have rolled away without us. I wouldn't have minded missing the train at the time so that I could stay with Anna a little longer, but I knew in my heart that that was not going to be possible. I turned to wave to her all the way down the platform and then leaned out of the window once we had boarded and were pulling away, craning my neck for one last look at her small figure disappearing into the distance as the steam from the engine settled on the platform between us.

My grandmother and I were very similar in appearance. She used to say that she saw her young self in me, maybe because we were both very sensitive and thoughtful in our characters, and we both liked writing poetry. I have older cousins who say they too can see the physical likeness now that I have reached the age that we all remember Granny Anna being.

At the time we left she still had Uncle Freddy and his family with her, although I knew that my cousin, his daughter, Marlies, didn't love her like I did. Soon, however, they would be gone too and she would be completely on her own. It was memories like those which were feeding the nightmares I was suffering from on our nights in the bomb shelter in Hampstead as the war we had been escaping from finally came to London.

As late as 1937 my father and mother decided we should return to Europe to visit Anna back in Reichenberg because they were becoming increasingly concerned about her health. I had recently received a worrying letter from her:

My Beloved Evchen,
Again a year has vanished without my being able to embrace you, my loved ones. Two and a half years you have been away from me. Health and all good wishes for 1937. Your old oma is not well health wise. In thought a very heartfelt New Year.

When they told me about the trip I was beside myself with excitement at the thought of seeing her after so long apart. Claude was still with us in 1937 and the four of us travelled first to Muhren in Switzerland. Our parents must have been talking to other people along the way who had more first-hand experience of what was going on in Czechoslovakia, or perhaps they were reading things in the papers that worried them, because they changed their minds at the last moment and left Claude and me in a hotel in Muhren and went on together without us. This was deeply upsetting for me after having built up my hopes of seeing Anna again.

I think that going back was a big decision even for them but they played down their concerns for Anna in order not to frighten me any more than they had to. In fact at that stage I was more disappointed than frightened, having been so looking forward to seeing my grandmother again and still not fully realising the scale of any possible danger to any of us. My sadness at being left behind was lifted slightly on the morning that I came down to breakfast in the hotel and found my idol, the dancer and film star, Fred Astaire, sitting at the next table, but even that dreamlike encounter couldn't lift my spirits for long.

Anna was being very well looked after by her son, Freddy, and Czechoslovakia was still a safe haven, being so far away from the tyranny inside Germany. We returned to England but I had not been able to see my granny again. The situation in Europe deteriorated after that, especially when Hitler was allowed to march into and annex Austria without a fight. From then on we followed the news of the apparently unstoppable march of the German Army on the radio and in the newspapers. Opinion in England at that time was divided between those who believed that declaring war on Germany was our only hope of stopping their territorial ambitions and those who thought we should go for appeasement and do everything we could to avoid starting another war like the First World War, which had wiped out almost an entire generation of young men. My parents were firmly of the belief that however terrible war might be, Hitler could only be stopped by force and that sooner or later England would have to join in to protect itself from being invaded as well.

For my mother the move to England had meant making huge adjustments to her status and lifestyle. To begin with she had no help in the house at all and found it hard to have to do everything for herself. My father, on the other hand, was just as comfortable in London as he had been in Berlin. He made friends with interesting people like the famous filmmaker, Alexander Korda and his brother. He had even got to know the Elgar family when he bought Sir Edward's derelict Netherall Gardens home in 1935 from his daughter not long after the great composer died, with the intention of rebuilding it and selling it on. The house was just around the corner from where we were now living in a ground floor flat at 51 Fitzjohn's Avenue. While clearing out the attic my father found an old and very valuable violin hidden. It was an emotional episode for the Elgar family when my father arranged for it to be reunited with his daughter.

My father was endlessly intrigued by the English and they in turn seemed to be intrigued by him. His positive attitude to our new homeland rubbed off on me.

"The English policeman," he told me soon after we arrived, "is your best friend. Not like a German policeman."

I decided he was right when on my way to school, I first saw a London "Bobby" at the end of my road,

Fitzjohn's Avenue, holding the hands of two schoolchildren whom he was helping to cross the road. From that moment on I never felt frightened or insecure in England, even with the Nazi threat building up just across the Channel, but I often thought about my grandmother and wondered what terrible fate might have befallen her.

Certain that war would inevitably be coming to Britain as early as 1936 my father had reinforced the wine cellar of the new Elgar house and transformed it into an air-raid shelter, thinking that would add to its sales appeal. He had already knocked down the original house, rebuilding it together with three other houses on the huge site. When he showed the house, a year or so later, to the famous music hall star, Bud Flanagan (the other half of double act Flanagan and Allen), Flanagan saw the air-raid shelter and promptly stormed out with his wife, accusing my father of being a warmonger. In fact it was a blessing in disguise that the sale fell through because when the air raids did start we were able to walk the few steps round the corner and shelter safely in the cellar of our own house instead of having to sleep crammed in with the hundreds of poor folk seeking shelter on Hampstead's underground station platforms. The station was reputed to have the deepest underground shaft in London.

When the headmistress announced that Kingsley School was moving out of London in 1939 to the safety of rural Cornwall I absolutely refused to go with them. There was no way I was willing to be separated from my parents again. It was bad enough being separated

19

from Granny Anna and worrying every day about what could have happened to her: I couldn't have borne to be in that same situation with my entire family. I would have preferred to die with them in an air raid, if that was what was meant to be, than to be left alone in the world. My memory of being in Berlin on my own, not knowing where they were or what was happening to them, was still vivid and frightening. It made me all the more aware of how acutely my father and Uncle Freddy must be suffering from being unable to look after their own mother when she was living in such a dangerous place during such a cruel time. I prayed that I would never have to face a similar dilemma to the one forced on them when they had to leave her behind in Prague.

When I turned sixteen in 1940 I became a legal adult, which meant there was a possibility I would be interned on the Isle of Man as an enemy alien, an even more terrifying prospect than being evacuated to Cornwall. Just in time, however, the law changed and I was told I had to apply for an "alien's book" instead. This entailed my making an appearance on my birthday at Bow Street Magistrates Court in Mayfair so that I could be cleared of any suspicion that I might be a foreign agent. I was flanked by two huge policemen as I entered the courtroom as a possible spy, while my father waited nervously outside on a bench, my protector as always.

"Did you belong to the Hitler Youth?" the magistrate asked.

"No," I replied, indignant at the very thought but trying not to show it.

"Are you in touch with anyone in Germany?" he went on.

"No," I answered truthfully, silently thanking God that my father had had the foresight to ban me from writing any more letters to Lottie.

When my father was called into the courtroom the only question the magistrate had for him was ironic.

"Does she ever need a good spanking?" he enquired.

My father responded with a polite and relieved show of amusement and at the end of the hearing the Court granted me my alien's book and spared me the horror of an internment camp.

Once I had got used to the idea of its existence I didn't think a great deal more about the mysterious pocket-book over the following years. There were so many other things to occupy the mind of a young woman growing up in London at the time. I liked the idea that we had such a romantic tale in our past, but once I had thought about it I could see the sense of my father's warnings about keeping it a secret and not asking any more questions. How would it have sounded if I started telling my friends that I was descended from a Prussian prince? At best it would have sounded like the foolish fantasies of a romantic young girl, at worst it would have sounded boastful. And how could I have proved my story to any doubters anyway?

He was right, I decided, it was better to just forget about it and get on with our lives in Hampstead where we enjoyed as good a life as was possible in the austere days of the war.

CHAPTER TWO

Granny Anna – No News from Prague

By 1940, although we barely dared to talk about it, I shared my father's fears and sadness about Granny Anna. I had such wonderful memories of her, which were being kept vividly alive by the letters and cards she had been writing to me from Czechoslovakia after we first escaped to England. They were full of love but gave no clues as to what the future might hold in store for her now the Germans were occupying Prague and Uncle Freddy was in London with us.

"*To my beloved Evchen,*" she wrote in one (in German), which I still treasure to this day.

I send you the heartiest wishes, my most beloved child. I send you in spirit a thousand heartfelt kisses, enclosed that my little grandchild shall be forever happy and shall stay healthy in body and soul and that in life her choices will always be right. That she remains her parents' great delight and that God graciously guides the ways of her life

so that we will soon meet in peace again before
your Oma must leave this earth.

Your old true Grossmuttechen, Anna.

In another she wrote:

My beloved Evchen, how much I would like to see
you again my beloved child, and Claude. I cannot
describe the longing I have for you.

After the German invasion her letters began to arrive
via the Red Cross and not the normal post. They still
gave us no clues as to what might really be happening
to her or what terrors she might be enduring. She
wouldn't have wanted to burden anyone else with her
worries anyway, particularly not her granddaughter.

When the German Army invaded the Sudetenland in
1938, where Reichenberg was situated, Uncle Freddy
and the family had fled to Prague, with Granny Anna,
his wife Lotte, and his daughter. But it wasn't long
before the German troops were pouring into that city
too. So they had to escape the country extremely fast to
avoid capture. Uncle Freddy told me how he witnessed
the soldiers arriving in the Wenceslas Platz and knew
that they had to get away as quickly as they could, but
that he realised it would have to be without his mother,
my granny Anna. By that stage it was no longer possible
for a Jewish family to travel across the borders openly
and Freddy was forced to flee with his wife and
daughter on foot, using a secret escape route over the
border into Italy. They then journeyed on to join us in

London, where they settled. When they arrived without Granny Anna I was devastated. I had been so sure they would bring her with them and I could hardly bear the thought of her being the only one of the family left behind.

I was told that she had been quite adamant that she didn't go with them, insisting that she was too old and arthritic to make the trip and that she would only be a liability to them. Uncle Freddy had eventually given in, seeing that he had no choice and hoping that an old lady living on her own in a city as big as Prague would not attract the attention of the Nazis. She hardly ever went out any more anyway, he reasoned, so how would they even know she was there? With any luck she would be able to live out her days in peace and comfort if he could find her somewhere pleasant to live.

Whatever happened he knew he had to save his wife and child before it was too late, even if it meant he had to leave his mother to take her chances. Before he set out to Italy he went in search of an apartment for her in a good area of the city. A man called Dr Borakova agreed to take her in as a tenant in his attic flat in the Praha 6 district, which was an affluent area, containing most of the foreign embassies. If she was going to be safe anywhere, Uncle Freddy decided, this would be the place. He left her with as much money as he could find. Their final goodbyes between mother and son must have been heartbreaking for both of them, neither knowing if they would ever see the other alive again. For me the separation from Anna was profound: it felt as if part of my very being had just disappeared.

Without any warning, after June 1942, there were no more letters. As each day passed I became more frozen with fear and more inconsolable. We were left with nothing but silence and not knowing, which made space for the darkest imaginings to invade our thoughts and dreams. We all pretended to hope for a while that it was just the war interrupting the postal services, including the Red Cross's, but in our hearts I think we realised that something much worse had probably befallen her, although none of us wanted to put our fears into words and risk making them feel more real. I didn't know what to do. I felt so helpless. I wanted to do something, to talk to my father or my mother but I knew I couldn't. It wouldn't have been any use anyway because they didn't know any more than I did.

Although I was fearful for Anna, I was also consoled because I knew my father felt the same way. He must have been tortured all through this very difficult time by Anna's fate, just as I was. I knew that he worried about her every minute of every hour of every day, wondering if she was alive or dead, fearing that she might even at this moment be being arrested by the Nazis or suffering unknown horrors in Auschwitz. Even when her letters and postcards had been arriving they were taking so long to travel between countries it was impossible to tell if something awful had happened to her in the meantime. Part of him must have desperately wanted to hear her voice and see her face again, while the other part must have been telling him to be thankful that we were all safely in England. Such thoughts must have made him feel like he was being

CHAPTER
THREE

Meeting Emilie

I woke up on the morning of 1 May 1945, switched on the little wireless in my room as usual and heard the unbelievable news that Hitler was dead. At that moment, as the news sank in, I felt a deep emotional bond with the people of Britain, from Winston Churchill and the King all the way to our neighbours in Hampstead. I felt that I was finally free and the Nazi terror had been destroyed for good, leaving the world a safer and happier place. As far back as I could remember the horrible, threatening figure of Adolf Hitler had darkened my life and suddenly that dark cloud was lifted.

Since 1940 I had been working in the Medici Gallery in Grafton Street, just off Bond Street. I had been in charge of their mail-order business which included supplying the royal family at Buckingham Palace, in particular the old Queen Mary. As well as meeting members of the European royal families I also got to meet other famous names like Winston Churchill's wife, Clemmie, and the Hollywood star, Danny Kaye. I loved the work and the hardest part of the day was having to make my way home on my own each evening in the blackout.

My relationship with my mother had matured steadily as I had grown up and we had become ever closer, with her treating me as an equal rather than a child. It seemed to me that her character had changed completely once she had become used to English life, and when she no longer had the responsibility and worry of bringing up children. We were becoming more like sisters as the years passed.

My brother Claude was away in the army when my father had told me about the pocket-book, having already been stationed somewhere out in the country. Soon he would become a captain in the Royal Engineers, and would be sent on active service in India, where he remained for the rest of the war. He had studied architecture, following in the footsteps of our distinguished father, and had narrowly missed being interned for the duration of the war as an enemy alien. After the war he followed the family tradition by becoming an architect and in 1950 he emigrated to Toronto, Canada with his new wife Inge, contributing extensively to the building of the city.

By then I had already married. I met Ken Haas for the first time at my cousin Freddie's 21st birthday party in North London in 1946. Ken had also fled from Germany before the war, just as we had, so we shared many of the same experiences. He had impressed me immediately. He was a powerfully built and athletic man, not tall, but tough both physically and in spirit. He was 38 and I was 21 and I was instantly captivated by his forthright, spontaneous manner. He worked for a family firm of goldbeaters, George M. Whiley, in the West End of London, who made stamping foils. He was a good businessman and as their export director he built the company up over the years, eventually moving it into substantial factory premises in Ruislip.

It was love at first sight and I married Ken in 1948, embarking on a long and happy partnership of more than forty years and producing three healthy sons, Anthony, Timothy and David. Ken was loving and devoted and you certainly could never grow bored in his company. Because of his job he was away travelling, sometimes up to five to six months of every year, which I found hard but in a way perhaps it strengthened our relationship even more. Bringing up three young boys, often on my own, there was little or no time to worry my head with romantic notions about who my ancestors might or might not have been: my attention was fully occupied in dealing with the complications of each day as it came, and planning for our family's future.

In 1955 tragedy struck my family again. My father, a heavy smoker, was diagnosed with cancer. He was just 65 and it seemed too early to lose him. But lose him we did when he died nine months later in March 1956. I was devastated by the loss and I was far from being the only one. He was a greatly loved public figure and many wanted to mourn his passing. Our local paper, the *Hampstead & Highgate Express*, wrote a headline article announcing his death and the time and place of his funeral. It never occurred to any of us that by doing that they were also advertising the fact that my parents' flat would be empty for at least a couple of hours while we were all at the crematorium in Golders Green. This allowed plenty of time for thieves to break in and turn out every drawer and cupboard in their search for hidden booty.

It is the cruellest thing to do, to invade the privacy of a family just as they are at their most vulnerable with grief. We walked in from the ceremony, my Uncle Freddy carrying the urn containing my father's ashes, just wanting to find some peace in which to compose ourselves after the ordeal, only to be confronted with a scene of total devastation. My mother's look of horror at this invasion of her life, just when she had to get used to the idea of living alone, was heartbreaking.

Believing that she might need someone there to support her, I followed my mother as she ran through to the bedroom, assuming that she wanted to check on some piece of family jewellery that might hold special sentimental value to her. But she seemed to have only one thing in mind as she ignored the clothes and other belongings strewn over the floor and headed for the dressing table. Rummaging through the debris she picked up a white envelope tied up with the green ribbon that I instantly recognised as being the one that held the ancient pocket-book. It was still in the same envelope from which my father had removed it the morning he had shown it to me sixteen years earlier.

"Thank God," she said, holding it to her heart as if that were the only possession that mattered to her in the whole apartment, a last precious piece of my father that she could still cling to now that she no longer had the man himself. Seeing the passion with which she hugged that elegant little book to her heart rekindled the curiosity I had felt as a young girl when my father first dangled that tempting snippet of a story in front of me. I wondered if she might be willing to pass the book on to me now that my father had gone. He had, after all, said that it would be mine.

"Mother," I ventured cautiously, "Father said I —"

"He also said not to go looking, Eve," she interrupted me, obviously guessing exactly what I was about to say, quickly composing herself, realising that she had allowed me to see too clearly how important the book was to her.

"But I —"

"It's just a notebook," she said, swiftly pushing the envelope back into its hiding place.

"Mother, please. I'm not a child any more. Why do you keep the book hidden away? What are you afraid of?"

"I'm afraid of you making a fool of yourself, poking around for answers that can't be found. The story ended with your grandmother. This talk of your father is upsetting me. Come on, let's go back to the others."

Realising this was not the moment to press her, I immediately fell silent, but our voices must have carried further than I realised because a little while later, once we had cleared up the worst of the mess from the robbery, my Uncle Freddy took me to one side and whispered out of my mother's earshot.

"Come round to my house tomorrow and I'll show you something."

That night I stayed with my mother in the flat, not wanting to leave her on her own after a day of so much emotional turmoil. It would be terrible for her to be lying awake on her own, listening to every sound, wondering if the thieves were returning, thinking about my father and the years that now stretched ahead without him. I wanted her to know that I would always be there for her when she needed me. The following day, unable to suppress my curiosity a moment longer, I took a train to Norbury in South London to visit Uncle Freddy.

"This is what I wanted to show you," he said, once he was certain I was comfortable, almost nonchalantly handing me a miniature painting of a pretty, auburn-haired young girl. She was wearing a formal red dress that showed off her shoulders despite an attempt by the artist to hide them with an artfully placed gossamer-like white shawl. This was such a profound moment for me after so many years of allowing myself to indulge in occasional romantic daydreams, before forcing myself to push those thoughts out of my mind in case they encouraged me to make a stand and try to get to the bottom of my family mystery once and for all. As I stared at the picture, mesmerised by her beauty, it felt as if Emilie were beckoning me into her life. Her soulful eyes stared directly at me from the tiny picture frame, a slight smile playing on her delicate lips, giving her an innocent, questioning look.

"That's her," he said, seeing my gaze locking on to Emilie's face.

I could never have imagined what a powerful effect that tiny portrait would have on me. In that instant I knew that this girl wouldn't be easy to let go, not easy at all. Uncle Freddy had lost me for a while but after a few moments my attention returned to the room and I became aware of what he was telling me.

"This is Emilie Gottschalk. She was your great, great grandmother, the one to whom Prince August wrote the dedication in the notebook that your mother has."

I remembered my father mentioning that his brother had a portrait of Emilie, but actually seeing this pretty little face peeking out at me suddenly revived all the curiosity I had felt as a young girl when he first told me the story.

"What do we know about her?" I asked, hypnotised by the sight of this young woman who was my direct ancestor and who had lived at the very heart of the Prussian Court at a time when it was central to European history.

"All we know is that she was young when she met the Prince, only fifteen years old. He on the other hand was in his fifties by then and was already an enormously wealthy, powerful and famous man. Despite the age gap it was a great love match. They stayed together for eleven years until he died. We believe she was the daughter of a Jewish tailor and we know that she and the Prince had a daughter, Charlotte, who was my mother's mother. Your father and I knew our grandmother Charlotte in our childhood, and she used to tell us things, dropping tiny hints that we never really understood. But that is all we know and it is just not possible to find out any more."

It sounded like the perfect fairy tale, the simple young tailor's daughter who captured the heart of a great prince, like a sort of Prussian Pygmalion, but I couldn't understand why everyone in the family kept stressing that these few facts were all that was known about the story. Surely a real-life fairy tale like this would have been talked about and written about in court papers of the time, and in history books ever since.

"Is that really all we know?" I asked, still without taking my eyes off her young face.

"We do have this," he went on, passing me an elderly sepia photograph of another woman, middle-aged and stately of build, dressed like Queen Victoria. "This is Charlotte, Emilie's daughter, and Anna's mother. She was my grandmother and your great grandmother."

I felt a catch in my throat as I tried to speak, remembering my grandmother again, who I had last seen waving to me and my brother on that railway platform in Prague. The photograph seemed to revive all the nightmares and fears I was storing at the back of my mind.

Uncle Freddy was gazing at the picture with the same intensity that I was. "Charlotte once said to your father, when he was still quite small, 'I am really a Duchess, you know, and I only ever travel anywhere first class.' And we both heard her talk about memories from when she was very little, when she told us she used to play wild games on the floor of a grand room somewhere in Berlin, with her father who was 'a great prince'. She kept saying that 'her whole life had changed completely' when she was five, but that was all she would ever tell us. If we tried to question her any further she would fall silent, almost as though, even as an older woman, she was still very reluctant to say more, or as if she didn't really know herself what had happened between her parents when she was a small child."

I went back to staring at the portrait, imagining the young girl sitting for the artist, trying to take in the fact that I was viewing the result of his handiwork more than 140 years after his brush strokes had dried. I was secretly hoping that if I stared hard enough at her face, Emilie's spirit might reveal some clues as to what had happened to her and the other members of her family that could have led to Anna's final predicament in Prague, whatever that might have been.

"What about the rest of the Gottschalks?" I asked, trying to piece the whole story together in my head and make sense of it. "Where is the family? What about their other descendants?"

"They don't exist," Uncle Freddy said. "When Charlotte married their name completely disappeared."

"Didn't anyone think that was a bit strange?"

He shrugged. "There wasn't much we could do about it. There are no records, no papers. There is just this picture and the pocket-book which my brother received. A lot of Jewish families have disappeared in

Europe over the last century for one reason or another."

I left Uncle Freddy's house that day feeling inspired. Now I had a clear picture of Emilie in my head and I knew for certain that she had existed. I also knew that she and Prince August had been devoted to one another and lived together for eleven years until his death, but frustratingly that was all I knew. It was another unfinished family story, like the mystery of what might have happened to Granny Anna. Again I went back to my normal daily life, allowing the tale of August and Emilie to slip to the back of my mind. If my parents and my uncle were all in agreement that the story should be allowed to rest then who was I to argue with them? I certainly didn't want to upset my mother by going against her wishes. From time to time I would remember the story, but over the coming years I was too busy being a wife and mother to give too much thought to an event that had taken place more than a century before.

CHAPTER
FOUR

The Call to Adventure

My mother continued living on her own in the same flat for another fourteen years after my father died. She was a fighter. Like Anna she too had arthritis in her hip. Operations had only just started in those days and were not as easy or reliable as they are today, so she limped around slowly, sometimes in great pain. Despite this, she always managed to visit us in Highgate regularly and her passing left a great void in my life. Her 77th birthday celebration on 4 October 1969 was a wonderful family occasion, but sadly it would be her last. Soon a burst ulcer, followed by a stroke, meant a six-month stay in Hampstead's New End Hospital, which was where she remained until she died on 24 April 1970. I visited her bedside virtually every day and I was 46 years old when she finally passed away. By now I was living in Highgate in my second family home since moving out of the Fitzjohn's Avenue flat, which had been my mother's home for the past 36 years since we had fled Berlin.

Before I even opened the front door I knew instinctively that the memories inside could easily swamp me if I let them. But my job that day was to sort out my mother's possessions in preparation for selling the flat and I knew I must stick to it, however hard the task might be. I felt I somehow owed it to both my parents to uphold the family tradition of stoicism.

The moment I stepped over the threshold I found myself drawn straight to the front room, where we had breakfasted on that day 28 years earlier when my father had presented me with the revelations about my family's past and where we gathered after my father's funeral amidst the chaos of the burglary. I paused in silent memory and looked around, drinking in the many familiar details of my younger life.

Although I had often asked my mother about the pocket-book after my father's death, she had always refused to hand it over. Now I prayed that it was still lying in the cupboard where I last saw her place it after my father's funeral fourteen years before. My fear was that she might have thought better of it and hidden it somewhere else, hoping perhaps that it would lie undiscovered. Or, worst of all, was it possible that she had destroyed it? I pushed such negative thoughts aside, took a deep breath and headed for the bedroom.

The old oak dressing table was still there, in the same place near the window where it had always been. I felt like I was treading on hallowed ground. The urge to see the book again was suddenly overwhelming. I pulled out the first drawer and rummaged a little, but there was nothing. Then the next one. Oh my God! There it was, still in the same yellowing envelope, tied up with the same piece of green ribbon. Thirty years after my father first told me that I would be the next keeper of the family secret, it had finally reached my hands.

Opening the envelope with a slightly shaky hand I gingerly slid the pocket-book out, sitting down to read the inscription that the Prince had written with the very pencil that still remained attached to the book. At last it had come to me and the feeling was overpowering. The small book was finally passing on to a new generation just as my father had wanted. I was excited and, above all, I was honoured that I had been chosen to become the guardian of this "forbidden fruit", our mysterious family legacy.

I carefully turned over the pages, studying each one. The words on the inside pages after the Prince's inscription must have been written by Charlotte, Anna's mother, when she was still probably very young, perhaps during the years just after her life "changed dramatically", as she had told my father and uncle when they were boys. The childishly written words were still as clear as when I first glimpsed them at the breakfast table with my father, even though they had been scribbled in pencil, the same little metal pencil that I had just pulled out from its place in the spiral spine of the book, its home for over a century. I actually tested it. It still worked after all those years. I put it back and pored over Charlotte's words again.

"*My beloved mother gave me a new dress at Whitsun . . .*" said one note. "*This book belonged to my beloved mother,*" read another and there were other hurried jottings about appointments and daily chores, some quite lengthy; giving tiny glimpses into this mysterious and vanished world, written by a little girl who had no idea what life held in store for her or for her future children and grandchildren, a girl who apparently didn't even fully understand what had happened in her own past. Perhaps she did know and was sworn to secrecy. Or was she hiding some terrible secret?

As I sat there in the silence of the empty flat, surrounded by all the familiar furnishings and belongings that I had known all my life and the smells I had breathed in every day as I grew up, I experienced an overwhelming urge to know more about Emilie and Charlotte. I wanted to find out why they and the rest of the Gottschalk family had been expunged from history, only allowed to live on in the oral stories of our family, as if they were some sort of guilty and dangerous secret from the past. I wanted to meet these two other women who had held this book in their hands and hear their stories, or to at least read them. I wanted to find out how this romantic sounding prince came to be with a Jewish tailor's daughter.

I took a taxi home that late spring evening, lost in thought. I didn't make much of the pocket-book find to Ken when I got in. In fact I played it down, simply explaining the few details that my father and Uncle Freddy had told me. I could see that he was having trouble taking the whole story in, but he offered to look after the diary for me and put it away in a safe place. I was happy for him to do that because I knew I needed some time to think about what I wanted to do next. Now that I had become the custodian of this extraordinary piece of history, what should my game plan be? The boys would have to be told about the heirloom, just as I had been all those years before, but perhaps not yet.

There seemed to be so many unanswered questions. Why did my mother never let me have the little book while she was alive? She was sitting right there the day that my father said he wanted me to have it, so why would she have hesitated for even a second to give it to me once he was gone? I couldn't understand it. Now she had left us, poor soul, I didn't feel comfortable with the idea of taking advantage and going against her wishes. And the idea of disobeying my father still seemed out of the question. I struggled to push away the urges I was feeling to do something about the book.

But time marches on once a life has ended and there was so much to do and much more to distract me, so again I let the pocket-book slip to the back of my mind. The pain of my mother's final battle still hurts even today as I think about her and my father and everything they did for Claude and me. If it hadn't been for Father's foresight, I wouldn't be here. We would have perished in Europe just like so many millions of other Jews. I still had no way of knowing for sure what had happened to Granny Anna. As far as I knew she had disappeared without trace, just like Emilie and her Gottschalk family. It was all so very strange and unsettling.

Three years passed, the sadness of loss softened and one day it felt like everything had changed. Having recently retired, Ken was busying himself with consultancy work. At 60 he was still fit and healthy and bursting with plans for the future. The boys had their own lives; Anthony was 23, Timothy 20 and David 13. I had more time on my hands and more space in my mind for old thoughts to rise to the surface. One day I decided to retrieve the pocket-book from Ken's cupboard and to seek refuge with it for a few hours, sitting at my bureau in the spare room upstairs. The moment I opened the delicate book and turned over each yellowing page, I felt my grandmother reaching out to me down the years. It was as if the book were our conduit, our link to one another; it felt as if she were beckoning me on to do something. I instinctively knew then that it was time for me to act, to dig deep and excavate our family's past, but I realised that whatever I did, I wouldn't be able to do it without the help and support of my family.

Mother had never discussed Anna's fate with me, nor anybody else as far as I knew. Anna's Red Cross letters had stopped coming in spring 1942, that was the last I knew or had heard. Had she died in Auschwitz with millions of others? Was she so fragile she didn't even make it to the camps? We knew that all food was scarce and she had little money. The pocket-book was only safe because she had passed it to my father before she left Berlin for Czechoslovakia. She need not have done that, she could have held on to it like my mother did. It wouldn't have been in my hands now if she had. I felt like it had come to me for a reason and I wondered if maybe Anna wanted me to have it eventually. Whatever the truth of it, I owed it to her to find out what lay behind the fairy-tale. My father's words took on a whole new meaning now. The more I thought about them the more I felt compelled to find out why nothing was written, why nothing existed, and this little pocket-book was all I now had to go on.

I felt torn in half but unable to talk about my dilemma to anyone. I knew that Ken believed I should obey my father's wishes and not go hunting for more information, and I didn't feel I could talk to my sons about it without imposing the same strictures on them that my father had placed on me. It was as if the secret could not be passed on to a new generation without the same strings being attached. My thoughts were in a turmoil as I remembered clearly how both my mother and my father had expressly urged me not to look into the family history and how my Uncle Freddy had repeated the fact that there was nothing more to find. I had never even considered disobeying any instruction that my father gave me in the past. But they were all gone now, I reasoned, all three of them, just like Anna and Charlotte and Emilie, all of whom must have been instructed to guard the family secrets in just the same way, although I couldn't imagine why that might have been.

Things were different in Europe from the time when my father first gave me the warning. I had grown used to living a safe and secure life in London, I was not fearful of the consequences of lifting a few stones to see what might lie underneath. It didn't seem possible to me that there wouldn't be some clues hidden away somewhere in the files, which would explain what had happened in my family's past.

More than a century of European history and upheaval had gone by since the events around the pocket-book had unfurled, surely it was all history now. What harm could possibly come from trying to uncover a few hidden facts, just for the record? I was a mature woman in my forties, I told myself firmly, who was capable of making my own decisions about such things without asking for the permission of my parents. It was the 1970s after all, and we no longer lived in the dangerous times that they had had to endure and that had shaped their characters to make them so cautious about everything. We were living in a safe and tolerant country where freedom of information and freedom of speech were amongst our most prized entitlements. It was time for these secrets to be uncovered and for a light to be shone into the goings on of the Prussian royal family in order to see what had led to their creation.

I knew absolutely nothing about Prussian history for that period even though it was where my family had sprung from. What sort of life would Emilie have led, having been catapulted right into the heart of such an exalted royal family at such a young age? And what could it have been like for her child to be forced to return after such a life to what appeared to be obscurity? I believed that these women had been ignored and forgotten for long enough. I was indignant on their behalf and felt it was my duty to go looking for them and to tell their stories to the world, if the world was interested in listening. Anna, my grandmother, had almost certainly been murdered by the Nazi killing machine and she, as much as her mother and grandmother, deserved to have her family story told. In one of the last letters my granny wrote to me from Prague she had wished that I would be guided to "make the right choices", and I felt a growing conviction taking hold that this was the right choice. I didn't exactly know what was guiding me to follow this path, but it felt like it was the spirits of Emilie, Charlotte and Anna.

It took me a long time to pluck up the courage to break the news of my decision to Ken. I hoped to be able to convince him that once he had more time on his hands it would be fun for him to join me in the hunt. I told myself it would give him something new to focus on, even though I knew in my heart that he had a deep reluctance about going back to anything that was to do with his past, including going to Germany itself. Like me he had been born in Germany and had had a difficult time escaping and getting his family to safety. I knew I was going to have to work hard to find a way of infecting him with my own enthusiasm for the project.

"That diary that I told you about," I said, as casually as I could one day. "The one that belonged to my great, great grandmother and had that inscription from Prince August in the front."

"Yes," he said, blissfully unaware of what I was leading up to. "Of course I remember you talking about it. I have it in my cupboard."

"I'm going to do some research into it."

"Into what?" Ken asked, more interested in reading his newspaper than in listening to whatever I was trying to tell him. "Your father said it was futile, didn't he? That there was nothing else there to be found."

"I've made an appointment for us to meet with an expert from Burke's Peerage," I confessed, hoping that if I said it fast enough he wouldn't object. "Tomorrow."

"What will that achieve?" he asked, finally giving up any hope of reading and lowering his paper in order to interrogate me more effectively.

"Well," I said, "they might be able to confirm if it actually is the Prince's handwriting in the inscription. And perhaps they could tell us a bit about his life and even something about Emilie. It seems worth a try."

"Very well," he said after a moment's thought. "I just hope you won't be disappointed, that's all."

I smiled to myself as he disappeared back behind the newspaper. I was sure if I could only find a way of catching his interest he would become as intrigued as I was. He just hadn't had time to think about it yet. I had called Burke's Peerage in the first place because I knew they were the world's greatest heraldic specialists and experts in the European aristocracy. They had been very helpful and given me the name of their heraldic expert, Jeffrey Finestone. Mustering all my courage, I had then called him.

"I have a diary that once belonged to Prince August of Prussia," I said, expecting to have to work hard to convince such a distinguished expert to show an interest, "which he has inscribed in his own hand."

"Prince August?" he said, the immediate excitement in his voice surprising me. "I would love to see that. Do please bring it to show me as soon as possible."

We had made a date to meet in his flat, which was not far from us in Hampstead. When the day came we found he had also invited a colleague, David Williamson, to hear my story. Mr Williamson was a man who used to appear on television as an expert in heraldic matters and genealogy; his expertise and knowledge covered handwriting and Prussian history. He said he would be able to give a second opinion and verify whatever might be said or seen. Realising that I was not going to be easily put off from my quest, and probably hoping that the experts would dismiss my foolish fancies out of hand so that he would be able to resume the peaceful retirement he had been looking forward to, Ken agreed to accompany me to the meeting despite his misgivings.

As soon as we arrived at Mr Finestone's elegant flat, he took the diary off me the moment we were through the door and sitting down. Turning it reverentially over in his hands he and his colleague squinted at it with barely disguised anticipation.

"Forgive me for being cagey," he said, "but I have been disappointed so many times before. Would you excuse us for a moment? We just need to check on something."

The two of them then disappeared into another room to study the book and confer in private, leaving Ken and me to wait in silence. When they came back in neither man could hide their glee.

"This is quite sensational," Mr Finestone bubbled. "We have investigated the handwriting in the inscription. It is indeed his handwriting, and your book would have belonged to him, the Prince August of Prussia, a member of the ruling Hohenzollern family and a nephew of Frederick the Great, the famous King. We can be quite certain of that. He would have written the inscription, although the actual signature would have been done by someone else. That would have been added by another hand afterwards. Such measures were often taken in those days to disguise and hide the truth of matters. It is this obsession with secrecy and disguise that makes historians' jobs all the harder, but in the end, of course, all the more fascinating. Do you know much about the Prince?"

"I have tried to find out a bit," I said, but he wasn't really listening, eager to show off his own knowledge of the subject.

"He wasn't just the youngest nephew of Frederick the Great, he is also the forgotten hero of the Napoleonic wars. He was an immense historical figure of his time, incredibly wealthy and a mighty warrior prince. It would be impossible to overstate how important and influential a man he was, and this is most definitely his handwriting. How on earth did you come to own such a rare gem?"

I explained the family connection and about how determined I had become to find out more about Emilie's life despite my parents' warnings that I would be wasting my time. They seemed to be amazed to find out about the liaison and an unofficial marriage. They didn't seem to know anything about the Prince's private life or about Emilie's existence or the fact that they had a child together.

"Well, Mrs Haas," he said when I had finished, "apart from Liechtenstein and the principality of Monaco, I can safely say that you are related to every royal family in Europe. Prince August, you see, was the great grandson of George I of England. You are also directly descended from Mary Queen of Scots and her son, James I."

At that moment I froze. What a revelation this was, but I didn't want to reveal any of my real feelings. Ken was standing right next to me, what was he thinking?

Then in his typical style Ken gave me a playful pinch. "I don't remember it being in the marriage contract that I was marrying a princess," he piped up.

"It's Emilie I'm really interested in finding, Mr Finestone," I reminded him, ignoring Ken's interruption. "And their daughter, Charlotte."

"Finding out anything about either of them will not be an easy task, Mrs Haas," he started gushing again, "not easy at all. At the end of August's life, in the mid-nineteenth century, all evidence of his past completely disappeared in the most mysterious circumstances. And of course now we have the problem of so much of the archive being stored behind the Berlin Wall in the East. It seems incredible that a man who must have had every aspect of his life written about in so much detail should simply disappear from the records, but that is exactly what happened. The East Germans absolutely refuse to cooperate in opening up their files. Historians from all over the world have been trying to find out about him throughout the last hundred years, with no success whatsoever. It is as if there were nothing written about him at all, yet he was one of the greatest Prussians who ever lived. It's quite possible the records have been destroyed but if there is anything still in existence no one has been able to find it."

"You must go to West Berlin, Mrs Haas. I urge you to visit the archive in Dahlem and beg them for help. You really must try and find out what happened to your great, great grandfather and grandmother. You have an extremely rare piece of history in your possession here. For Prince August, a leading member of the royal Hohenzollern dynasty, to live for eleven years with the daughter of a Jewish tailor simply cannot be explained."

"It's really just a family heirloom," Ken said when Mr Finestone eventually paused for breath. He was obviously not keen to see me being encouraged to go against my father's wishes to keep our family secrets low-key and private.

"Oh, it's much, much more than that, Mr Haas," Mr Finestone assured him. "This book belonged to the warrior prince. He fought and defeated Napoleon and became the wealthiest man in Prussia. Your wife could have the key that unlocks the whole puzzle. A puzzle which has defeated all the most learned historians in the world."

"If this were my diary," Mr Williamson chipped in, "I would be attempting to analyse it completely. I would want to find out everything I could about it."

"You really should make this public," Mr Finestone said.

"Absolutely," his friend agreed. "We would love to be part of it with you. Do please go public."

"My wife wishes this to be kept private," Ken jumped in, obviously surprised and realising for the first time just how significant the little book was. "She doesn't want the whole world to know her private family business."

"That's right," I assured them all. "It's only Emilie, my great, great grandmother who I am really interested in at the moment. I want to find out how she came to be in this position and what happened to her after the Prince died."

"Indeed. Anti-Semitism was almost official in Berlin at that time," Mr Finestone said. "For a Prussian prince to get together with a Jewish girl . . ."

He petered out, unable to find sufficient words to express the level of his amazement at such a thought.

"Do go to Berlin, Mrs Haas. I would if it were me. You have an extremely rare piece of history here. This is really exciting. You mustn't allow it to slip through your fingers."

I came away from that meeting high on excitement at the possibilities of the adventure that I could now see lying ahead of me. To have had the inscription verified as being from the hand of the Prince himself was an enormous step forward. It meant that the story my father had told me had not been a mere fairy tale, passed hopefully down the generations. I was genuinely linked to this great historical figure. He was my own blood, and I knew that now there would be nothing that could stop me from continuing my search. It was as if Mr Finestone and his friend had given me permission to set off on my quest. I put my father's warnings about not pursuing the truth to the back of my mind, reasoning that they had been made because he hadn't wanted me to make a fool of myself and from the perspective of a very different time in history, telling myself that Mr Finestone and his friend had more than confirmed that I wouldn't be doing that and that it was my duty to Anna and to posterity as well. If I didn't embark on this it was hardly likely that anyone else could or would and then the truth might never come to the surface. This book was genuine and it could hold the key to solving a great historical mystery. Without even asking him, I could tell that Ken was not nearly as keen as I was. I suspect that inside he was cursing Mr Finestone for giving me so much encouragement. I think he could see clearly that there was a danger that this hunt was going to take over both my life and his and that it could take us to dangerous places. He had been hoping for a quiet life after decades of working hard, the last thing he wanted was to stir up trouble for himself and his family.

"You have the diary," he said when I eventually forced him to tell me what was going through his mind. "Isn't that enough?"

I knew better than to argue. I needed to save my ammunition for later. My spirits were riding too high for me to be willing to be discouraged now and I told myself I would work out how to bring Ken on board later. I was intending to contact every possible expert I could think of to try to discover where this missing information had been buried and to work out how it had all been hushed up so successfully. Who, I wanted to know, had instructed that Prince August and Emilie should be erased from the history books, and why?

A few days after our visit to his flat, to my sheer delight I received a letter from Mr Finestone containing a neatly drawn up family tree written in his own hand. I could see my name linked directly to the Prince and Emilie and through them to the English and Prussian royal families. It was then that the penny really dropped. He obviously wanted to confirm in my mind just how important an historical item he thought the notebook was, although by then I didn't need any more encouragement to keep up the hunt. One of the first calls I made as soon as we got home was to the Central Archive in the Dahlem District of West Berlin, just as Mr Finestone had instructed.

"Prince August of Prussia?" the unemotional voice at the other end of the line said. "No, we have nothing."

I was surprised that he was able to tell me that so easily, without even having to go away and check, so I could only assume he had been asked the same question before and had already searched in vain. To counteract my initial disappointment I reminded myself that Mr Finestone had warned me that all information about the Prince was mysteriously missing. This reaction was therefore only to be expected. His excitement had temporarily led me to forget that the hunt for Emilie was not going to be easy; the call to Dahlem immediately set me straight on that. I was obviously going to come up against all the same brick walls as he and the other historians before him had encountered.

"The only place where they are likely to have anything," the bored voice continued, "is in the East, at their Merseburg archive. But the East Germans have helped nobody, and have blocked all attempts from the West to get access to their papers. We know that they have files on the Hohenzollern royal family but I cannot imagine that they will be willing to open them up for you."

The early 1970s were an era when the Cold War was still at its height with everyone in the West living under the two great perceived threats of communism and nuclear war, just as today we are persuaded to live in fear of terrorism and global warming. The very thought of having to have anything to do with the sinister East Germans was particularly chilling for people like Ken and me who had already escaped one totalitarian regime in our lives, but still I seized at this straw. If I didn't at least try asking the authorities in Merseburg, I would never know for sure what their response would be. With the help of the West German embassy I managed to get a telephone number for the Merseburg archive and dialled it nervously. It took a few minutes of clicking and buzzing before the line connected and the number rang. It continued to ring for what seemed like an age and I was on the verge of hanging up and trying again when an ill-tempered voice answered.

"Put your request in writing," the woman snapped as, with my heart in my mouth, I started to tell her what I was after — and then the phone line went dead. It seemed I had already exhausted her patience by daring to ask for her assistance.

Only momentarily discouraged by her surly response, I sat down and wrote them a letter as the woman had suggested, requesting a meeting and asking for access to their files. Even as I punched the words out on the typewriter I knew it was a triumph of hope over experience, but I wasn't about to let a single opportunity pass me by in my search. I posted the letter and resigned myself to having to wait some time for an answer.

Still unwilling to accept that there really was no information about Prince August anywhere in the Western world, I trawled every library I could find over the following months as I waited for a response from the East. Not even the British Library, which boasts that it has a copy of every book ever printed, was able to turn anything up. Every librarian I recruited to my cause started out fired with enthusiasm and certain they would be able to turn up some clue that would move me forward. But they all ended up coming back shaking their heads, as disappointed as I was at their inability to help unearth any more pieces of the puzzle.

"This is astonishing," the Curator of the British Museum said when I showed him the diary. "We would dearly love to exhibit this. Anything at all about Prince August is much sought after. We have been trying for years to find out about him ourselves. Prince August

55

living with a Jewish girl and bearing a child — what a sensation! You have no idea how anti-Semitic Prussia was at that time. It really is an extraordinary story. I wish you the best of luck with your search."

It was beginning to look like I was going to need all the luck I could get. I kept in touch with Mr Finestone for a while, telling him of any progress I might be making, however modest it might be, grateful for his continued encouragement and enthusiasm in the face of one disappointment after another. Tragically, he would never finish my journey with me, dying in 1981 when he was probably little more than 40 years old. It was a sad time for me. On some days, when I was particularly low, I felt like I was in danger of being swallowed up by my own guilty conscience about my father. I imagined that I too might be struck down by some invisible force for daring to even think of unravelling the mystery of the missing prince. I managed to force myself to put such superstitious foolishness from my mind. I couldn't afford to let anything discourage me from sticking to my purpose.

There was a small converted summerhouse at the top of our garden, which I took over as my office, sitting in there for hours, plotting and planning. I didn't care how long it took, I was determined to unravel the mystery of my family's past.

Now that the pocket book was with me and I was beginning my search, I so wished I could speak to my Uncle Freddy again. But Uncle Freddy had passed away in 1966 and he had left Emilie's miniature portrait in the safe hands of Alice, his second wife. She very kindly lent me the original as it occurred to me that if I could find an artist, maybe he or she would be able to paint an original copy from the master. My searches led me to an experienced portraitist called John Dudley, who agreed to take on the commission and executed it with such skill that it was hard to know which one was the copy. I returned the original to Alice, feeling thrilled with the result. Now I had my Emilie forever and I vowed never to let her leave my side. The little portrait became my lucky charm and I took her everywhere with me, occasionally taking a peep at her, if only to give me some inspiration when I was in need of it.

CHAPTER
FIVE

Return to Berlin

My letter to Merseburg in East Germany produced an unsurprising silence, but their lack of courtesy and cooperation only made me more certain that they were the ones who held all the secrets in their vaults and that if I could just persuade them to unearth them they were going to reveal the whole story. The ever-increasing layers of mystery, and the brick walls of silence that I kept coming up against, made me all the more determined to find a way to talk the East Germans into opening their archives up to me.

Aware that Ken and the boys may already be growing weary of my obsession — my constant talking about it and my gnawing frustration as I seemed to be going round and round in circles — I had been staying off the subject as much as possible at home, but the puzzle was still churning around in my brain every waking hour and often in my dreams as well, the unanswered questions eating away at me. I knew the moment was approaching when I was going to have to win Ken over to my cause fully and persuade him to come with me to Germany, a place that held a great many mixed memories for both of us, some happy, others both sad and terrifying.

"Let's go to visit the archive in Dahlem," I said breezily over breakfast one morning, hoping that if I talked fast enough he wouldn't have time to think of all the reasons why he didn't want to go. "We need to meet these archivists face-to-face if we want to win them to the cause. Then while we are there perhaps we can go over to the East and visit the archive in Merseburg."

I hoped I had said that casually enough not to alarm him, but there was no chance of that. If nothing else I had succeeded in gaining his full attention. It was now 1973 and more than three years after my mother had died and the pocket book had passed to me. We had been back to Germany a few times since the end of the war, the last time in 1966 when we had taken the children to see my family's flat in the Berlin suburb of Charlottenburg and my old school, both of which had miraculously survived the bombs and the post-war reconstruction. It had been an emotional experience, bringing back numerous long buried memories and I think Ken had hoped that I would accept it as providing a closure on that whole part of my life. This time however it was different. I was asking him to go into the Communist East and take on German officialdom there.

"Dahlem, OK," Ken sighed, looking up from the plate of food he had been attacking with gusto. "But Merseburg? Think carefully, Eve. Have you any idea what it was like for me getting my parents out of

Germany? Are you really asking me to go back in there again and face another dictatorship?"

Having already escaped from Nazi Germany to London, Ken went back to Frankfurt in 1938 in order to arrange false papers for his parents. He had previously worked at the Dresdner Bank as their youngest ever foreign exchange dealer and it was a director of the bank who had agreed to help him with the papers. Ken knew that the man was a leading local Nazi and could well betray him, but was forced to trust him. It was a chance he thought he had to take; there was no alternative, having no one else to turn to. Ken managed to obtain the papers for his parents and that night, when he was posting a letter, an anonymous passing woman warned him that he was in great danger. Miraculously Ken escaped safely back to England. I realised just how much I was asking of him by suggesting we go back.

"It's a different world over there now, Ken." I tried to make light of his worries, although I understood all too well just how much I was asking of him because the idea frightened me as well. The prospect of never being able to find out the truth about August and Emilie, however, was worse. I felt I had to take the risk and, selfishly perhaps, I didn't fancy taking it without Ken, my protector, at my side.

"Eve," he spoke patiently, as if trying to explain to a rather dim child the error of her ways, "the East is a totalitarian regime that tortures, spies on and incarcerates human beings for no reason. Ring any bells? You were born in East Germany. They could hold you there forever if they chose to. Just the thought of being within their reach is unbearable, don't you understand that?"

"We'll take Anthony as security," I said brightly. "He was born in England."

I was confident that our eldest son, who was 23 by then, would be up for a bit of an adventure. He had not had to live through the horrors of the war and the Holocaust and consequently had all the confidence of a young citizen of the modern world. He had recently won a Short Film Award at The National Film Theatre and was planning a career for himself in television and films, so I was sure he would be happy to spare us a few days of his time for a mission this interesting. Having a feeling that the adventure I was determined to embark on might end up becoming all consuming, I had called our three sons together at the beginning to tell them exactly what I was planning to do and why I wanted to do it. It was, after all, their heritage I was going to be investigating just as much as it was mine. Over the following months they had become almost as excited by the story of Emilie and Prince August as I had. Despite his reservations about the wisdom of the whole venture, I also knew that Ken would be there to support me once he realised I intended to go anyway and that I could not be talked out of it however hard he might try. I knew there was no way he would ever consider letting me go to such a dangerous place on my own.

Sure enough, a few weeks later Ken, Anthony and I arrived in West Berlin. At that time the western half of the city I had known as a child was a tiny, walled-off island of democracy, marooned in the East since the end of the Second World War and the division of the defeated German Empire between the victorious Allies. It was only accessible by air, every other access being walled off and heavily guarded to prevent anyone disenchanted with communism from escaping to the West. It felt so strange to be back amongst those familiar streets and buildings. Some I could still remember so clearly from my happy early childhood, and now it was so unnerving, knowing that we were surrounded on all sides by lands that were rigorously policed by a ruthless and all-powerful communist dictatorship. A walk down the Unter den Linden, the beautiful boulevard running up to the Brandenburg Gate, which should have brought back so many pleasant memories, now ended in rolls of barbed wire and the high blank face of the Berlin Wall which divided the East from West so brutally and symbolically. Everywhere we looked as we stood staring at this monstrosity we saw signs bearing skulls and crossbones predicting instant death for anyone who even thought of crossing over without all the right paperwork and permissions. It almost felt like I was being warned off from going any further with my hunt for the truth, as if the authorities were giving me one last chance to give up, turn back and go home before I had committed myself too deeply and was unable to put whatever genii I might be about to unleash back into the box.

The Director of the archive at Dahlem did not seem as pleased to see us as I was to see him. He reluctantly admitted that he was in charge of the Hohenzollern archive, and gave me the distinct impression that he believed I was just one more in a long line of gold diggers who had been knocking on his door over the years trying to prove their lineage in the hope of claiming some long-lost fortune or title. When he eventually listened to my story he must have been able to feel how passionate I was about the search and his suspicions seemed to subside a little, but not enough to make me think that he was really on my side. After a while he started to open up a little about the subject of the Hohenzollern family, perhaps secretly pleased to have a captive audience who was so passionate about a subject he had some expertise in.

"If the Prussian kingdom had survived," he explained, "Prince Louis Ferdinand would now be king."

"What about Emilie Gottschalk?" I asked, now that I at least had his attention. "What do you know about her?"

"I have never heard of her," he replied, a little disdainfully. Perhaps he didn't like having to admit that there might be a hole in his knowledge. Or perhaps he wasn't interested in any name that didn't carry a great title with it. "Prince August only had two women in his life," he added categorically, as if daring us to argue.

Two others? I knew so little about his life that even this snippet of information was news to me. "Who were these two women?" I asked.

"There was Friederike Wichmann, his first wife, who was bestowed with the title Von Waldenberg by the King when she married the Prince, and then his second wife, Auguste Arendt, who was titled Von Prillwitz. They were both morganatic marriages because the women were commoners who were given these titles by the King. The Prince's descendants from these two wives are still well respected families living in Berlin and have inherited these titles."

He made it sound like I was deliberately trying to upset the status quo and cause trouble for August's established heirs, or that I was trying to muscle my way into high society in some way, but I wasn't going to let his superior tone put me off now I had come all this way. I pulled out the miniature of Emilie and showed it to him.

"But you have never heard the name of Emilie Gottschalk?" I tried one last time.

"I'm sorry," he snapped irritably, hardly glancing at the picture. "I can't help you. Like I told you on the phone, you will need to go to Merseburg in the East. Any surviving papers of the Hohenzollern family will be there. But I wouldn't bother if I were you because the authorities won't allow anyone to access them. You need their permission just to go there, let alone have files opened for you. These are dangerous times, particularly if it is information you are looking for."

I hardly dared to look at Ken as we listened to the Director. I knew that these words of warning would have been reinforcing all the fears that he already had about crossing the border to the East, coming as they did on top of the warnings from my parents not to go looking for more information. It was sounding more and more like I was embarking on a wild goose chase but I knew I couldn't give up and go home now without at least trying to talk the East Germans into helping me. I knew in my head that what this man was saying was true and they would almost certainly turn me away at the door, even if they didn't arrest me, but in my heart I wanted to believe that there was always a chance that they would want to help me and would agree to open their files to us. I couldn't abandon Emilie's memory just because I had come up against a few obstacles. She deserved better than that.

"We have to go to Merseburg now," I said to Ken and Anthony the moment we were back outside the Dahlem building, trying to sound more confident about the idea than I actually felt.

"Evechen," Ken said, hardly able to hide his exasperation at my persistence, "it isn't safe. We can't visit the East. Come on, let's go home."

"The British Embassy will help us," I said, pretending I hadn't heard him. "Maybe the Consul will see us. Let's go and ask."

Probably imagining that the British Consul might be able to make me see sense even if he and my parents couldn't, Ken agreed reluctantly to come with me to talk to him. It wasn't hard to get in to see the Consul, who listened calmly and politely to what I had to ask. Ken and Anthony remained quietly in the background, allowing me to do all the talking. The Consul was obviously intrigued and stared at the pocket-book intently as he listened, turning the pages thoughtfully, hearing me out to the end.

"The British Government has no diplomatic representation in the East," he reminded me when he realised what I was actually hoping to do next. "I'm very much afraid you cannot go over to the East, Mrs Haas. You were born in Breslau, in East Prussia and the authorities over there will be aware of that. They seem to know pretty much everything about anyone who crosses their borders. If they chose they could stop you from leaving. They could arrest you on some trumped-up charge and put you in prison without even informing us. There you would remain and we would be helpless to do anything for you from this side. We probably wouldn't even know where they had taken you. Besides you can't just turn up at the archive and expect them to welcome you with a cup of tea. Where is your invitation? Do you have one?"

His tone was so reasonable and his words were so final I felt a terrible sinking feeling in my stomach. Maybe I wasn't going to be able to do this after all. Just when I was about to give up and politely thank him for taking the time to hear me out, I heard my husband's voice beside me sounding strong and firm, coming to my rescue like the white knight he always was.

"We have a letter," Ken said, passing a copy of my letter to Merseburg across the desk. I felt a wave of optimism pervading my thoughts, and gratitude towards him for speaking up on my behalf, especially since I knew he was even more anxious than the Consul to discourage me from this mission.

"But this is your letter to them requesting an invitation," the Consul said after a quick scan of the letter. "It's not an invitation."

"Correct," Ken nodded, as if that were obvious but irrelevant.

"It's all far too dangerous," the Consul said, shaking his head and returning the letter. Ken slid it back in his pocket.

I knew that although the Consul was duty bound to say all these things to cover himself in case anything went wrong, he couldn't actually stop me from doing anything I wanted as long as I wasn't breaking the law. I was a citizen of a free country and, as long as I was in West Berlin, I was still in a free country. If I wanted to put my own life in danger that was my business and no one else's. It wouldn't be that bad, I told myself. I decided I had no option but to continue ignoring everything that had been said to me.

"Well I would like to give it a try," I said to the room in general. "So how do we go about it?"

The Consul continued to try his best to change my mind, until eventually he realised, as Ken must have done, that there was nothing he could say to deter me and so he had better advise me as well as he could in the hope of limiting the potential damage. He let out a deep and prolonged sigh.

"From the first moment that you enter the East, Mrs Haas," he said, "be very, very careful. You must report first to the Reise Bureau on Alexanderplatz, a so-called 'tourist office'. If by some miracle they grant you official permission to travel to Merseburg it is a journey of about forty miles. Even if they do give you permission it will only be for one day and they will insist that you are back at Checkpoint Charlie, the crossing point for foreigners between East and West Berlin, by 8 p.m. sharp on the same day. When you are safely back through to the Western side report to the French, American or British soldiers on duty and tell them that I must be informed. They will contact us immediately. Be safe and good luck."

CHAPTER
SIX

Crossing the Border

As we walked out of the embassy I set a brisk pace, staring straight ahead, hardly daring to catch Ken's eye. I knew that he had given up hope of dissuading me and when we got to the car I gave him a big hug and told him how delighted I was for the way he had supported me in the Consul's office, although I knew that didn't mean he wouldn't be cross with me for forcing him into this corner with my stubbornness. I knew that now he had accepted that I was going to go to Merseburg he would be behind me every inch of the way and I loved him deeply for that. There was no way he would ever have let me go on a mission like that alone.

I also knew that Ken would be the best possible ally to have if we got into any trouble; he had proved that many times in his life. When he finally escaped from Hitler's Germany he was on a train with many other Jews also fleeing the regime. The train was stopped before it reached the German border and the SS came swaggering on board, demanding to see everyone's papers and ordering all the Jews to disembark. Ken knew that anyone who did so would be taken into custody and that if he allowed that to happen he would never get any more chances to escape. He noticed all the other passengers were behaving with a humble politeness towards the strutting, bullying young SS officers and he decided to try a different tactic.

When they burst into his compartment he looked up angrily from his newspaper as if hugely irritated at having his peace and tranquillity interrupted. Despite the fact that his heart was thumping with fear he barked at them angrily, demanding to know what they meant by disturbing him so rudely, ordering them to leave him alone immediately so that he could continue reading his paper in peace. Taken aback by being confronted by an aggression even greater than their own, and brainwashed to obey orders like any good soldiers, the young officers were thrown into confusion and backed away, concentrating their efforts on the many others who were not putting up any sort of fight and were showing the levels of fear and humility that the officers expected.

Ken went back to staring at his paper while every other Jew was taken off the train and it was allowed to rumble on its way across the border to freedom. His was exactly the sort of courage and bravado I was likely to need on my side in the task that lay ahead of me and I knew I would need to cajole him a little in order to get him to do what I wanted. It meant so much to me that he was such a great support, even when he thought it went against his better judgement, and I told him so. He wasn't a man for showing his emotions — like many men of his generation and background he held a lot of it in. I protected my emotions as well, like most people who had lived in Hitler's Germany, and I had learned to be careful when displaying them in front of Ken. He was a pragmatic man, always believing in the value of facts over feelings. He was the kind of person who believed the business of life was to go forwards and to "let sleeping dogs lie" when it came to the past. I understood how difficult it was for him sometimes to accept my point of view and appreciated him all the more for going along with it. Because of the understanding we had for each other we were always on equal terms, despite his sometimes overly self-protective and cautious nature. His enthusiasm, once it had been ignited, was immense. He was a man who charged on through life, regardless of any obstacles put in his way.

We rose at dawn the next morning, wanting to get as much time as possible on the other side of the wall and headed for Checkpoint Charlie in a hired Mercedes, with Anthony driving. An American soldier on duty on the western side politely asked us to draw up while he studied our passports. I already felt nervous, frightened we were going to be stopped and sent back before we had even got across to the other side. After what seemed like an age, the guard handed back the papers and nodded us through. We moved gently across the no-man's land between East and West towards the next barrier, already noticing that the scenery was changing around us. So many of the buildings were boarded up and falling into disrepair and road surfaces were cracked and potholed. These streets had once been as much a part of the beautiful, prosperous city I had been brought up in as the ones in the western sector that we were leaving, but it looked like the area had had its heart eaten out and that nobody had cared for it or had the money or will to maintain it.

We crossed the barrier that signalled entry to the East, and almost immediately we were instructed to report on foot to the registration desk in a nearby building. We did this dutifully, without any fuss, and returned to our Mercedes before travelling on to the Reise Bureau, on the Alexander Platz. Our venture could easily fall flat on its face at this point. Our fate would be in the hands of whatever petty official waited inside. We needed to get a permit to travel on and to return to the West later. Ken, suddenly in his element, took charge, just as I had hoped he would once the chips were down. We parked the car and climbed out, aware already that we were being watched by the armed and unsmiling East German soldiers standing guard all round the area.

"Don't say anything," he whispered as we walked into the shabby office. He informed the man behind the desk where we wanted to go as though this was the most normal request in the world and that he had no doubt it would be granted.

"Merseburg?" the arrogant young official looked at us incredulously. "Have you an invitation?"

"Yes, we have." Ken lied with such confidence he almost convinced me we had. He waved a copy of the letter I had written to the archive, just as he had waved it in front of the Consul. "We're expected," he said, seeming impatient at being held up even for these few minutes when he had important business to attend to. "It's all arranged."

The man glanced at the letter but, unlike the Consul, didn't bother to read it. Maybe Ken's confident manner was enough to convince him that it was indeed a letter of permission. Without the slightest hint of a smile he issued the day permit and warned us, just as the Consul had, of the danger we would be in if we didn't comply with the conditions.

"You will be arrested," he said handing the passports and letter back, "if you are not out of the East by eight o'clock tonight."

Hardly daring to even look at one another we took the papers from him and walked briskly outside, still aware of the many sets of eyes following our progress. We climbed back into the car and drove off before he had a chance to change his mind. My heart was thumping in my ears and I felt uncomfortably conspicuous. The plush Mercedes with its unfamiliar West Berlin number plates looked completely out of place, drawing stares from nearly everyone we passed, some curious and some suspicious or even downright hostile. It seemed endemic, and a part of the character of the East for varying reasons, that no one dared to smile. There was no chance that our progress was going to go unnoticed that day: every official who needed to know would be informed of every move we made.

The bleak landscape continued to unravel along the side of the road as the Mercedes purred past. The city of Merseburg had suffered terribly in the war, losing around 65 per cent of its population. It seemed like all the clocks in the land had been stopped thirty years earlier, reinforcing the sinister reputation that the secretive East Bloc had in the West. His fingers so tight on the steering wheel his knuckles were turning white, Anthony stuck meticulously to the speed limit; the last thing we wanted to do was give the police any excuse to pull us over and demand to see our paperwork. Any hitch like that could end up delaying us for the whole day or might even precipitate the arrest that the Consul had warned us about.

An hour after leaving Checkpoint Charlie the high white walls of a medieval castle loomed up on the horizon ahead of us.

"That's the archive," Ken said, and I felt a knot of excitement tighten inside me. Maybe, just maybe, somewhere behind those forbidding walls rested all the secrets I wanted to gain access to. If August, Emilie and Charlotte's stories did lie hidden in files somewhere in there, as I suspected they did, all we had to do was persuade the archive's guards to allow us access. Despite the levels of hostility that had greeted us from the few officials we had dealt with so far, I still felt optimistic that if we just refused to give up we would eventually persuade someone to help us. They couldn't all be embittered, brainwashed, frightened automatons, could they?

CHAPTER
SEVEN

At the Castle Walls

We drew up at a small outhouse beside the road, which seemed to be the guardhouse to the castle. I stepped out of the car with Ken, who was exhibiting the same confidence he had shown at the border. Anthony sat impassively in the car, staring straight ahead, his expression carved in stone so that we didn't give anything away.

"What do you want?" a young looking woman asked us from inside the hut. "What have you come for?"

"We have an appointment," I said.

"Who have you come to see?"

Ken wasn't saying a word. He replied with a silence, as if angry with the woman for even daring to challenge us, thrusting our British passports towards her as if that should explain everything.

"Oh, I know," she said, apparently pleased with herself for being able to show off her efficiency and knowledge of the system, "it's Frau Steglitz you want."

"Yes," Ken nodded curtly, as if he had been testing her and was impressed by her response, but still not giving way to a polite smile, as he would have done in a normal, relaxed conversation in England. "That is correct."

Without hesitating, the woman rang through to some unseen authority behind the castle walls to inform them that three British people had arrived at the gates with an appointment to see Frau Steglitz. To our amazement she slammed down the telephone receiver with a curt, "Gut".

Ken waved to Anthony to leave the car and join us as the woman showed us through a small side door. I hardly dared breathe for fear of upsetting our good luck.

"What next?" I whispered into Ken's ear once we were inside but he said nothing.

Another stony-faced official was approaching us. She seemed perplexed, eyeing us up and down.

"Come with me, please," she said.

The décor was grim and austere. What dark secrets did these plain walls hold, I wondered? The woman marched us into a room then turned to face us.

"My name is Frau Steglitz," she said, "now why have you come here?"

She seemed discomforted by our appearance from nowhere. Her attitude was confrontational and far from welcoming. Everything about her, from her short-cropped hair to the way she stood before us with her shoulders squared up, screamed hostility. It was obvious, she thought we had ambushed her, had invaded her kingdom. No doubt during the long years of the Cold War she had been given as much reason to fear the citizens of the West as we had been given to fear the East and here we were, East meeting West, having by-passed all the protocols which she had been brought up to believe were essential.

"What is your business here?" she snapped.

Ken thrust our passports towards her again, determined not to be intimidated. She glanced at them but didn't seem as impressed by them as the guard outside had been.

"I sent a letter," I said, my voice sounding much less certain in my ears than Ken's had.

"Eve Haas," Ken barked by way of an introduction, as if hoping that just mentioning my name should be enough to guarantee her cooperation. "We wrote to you from London."

"Yes, I know," she replied without a flicker of an expression. "Follow me."

Frau Steglitz led us through to another very basically furnished room and nodded for us to sit on the rickety-looking wooden visitors' chairs while she went round behind her desk to assume her position of authority over the meeting. Her attitude was that of a headmistress who had summoned us to appear in front of her to answer for some misbehaviour or other.

"So, you received my letter?" I asked nervously.

"Yes," she nodded, still giving nothing away.

"What was your reply?" I ventured after a few awkward moments of silence.

"The reply is in the post," she said. "You will receive it when you get back to England."

"We are here now," I said emphatically, following Ken's firm lead, feeling I had nothing to lose by pushing my luck. "I am looking for my great, great grandmother. She had a liaison with the Prince August of Prussia and I want to look her up in the archives."

"Oh, that is absolutely impossible," she snapped. "Absolutely no one can enter our archives here. It is not permitted. We receive requests from eminent American professors all the time and we always refuse them. No one can come here from the West to research. It is not allowed."

The very idea that we would have the nerve even to ask seemed to be beyond her comprehension. Since we were at least inside the castle walls and she didn't appear to be about to call the guards to have us ejected or arrested, I decided to persevere.

"They lived together for many years and had a baby —"

The mention of the word "baby" seemed to infuriate her and she immediately started shouting.

"A *baby*?" she boomed, slapping her palms on the desk and making us all jump. "I don't know why you people in the West are so impressed with babies. People have babies all the time, every minute and second of every day all over the world. Why should you worry about one baby? Just because you once had an Empire you think you can study in our Archive. Well, it is certainly not possible."

"How could it be made possible?" Ken asked, apparently not intimidated by her sudden explosion of anger.

78

"You would have to get permission," she told him, as if such a possibility were out of the question, and obviously hoping her tone was enough to end the whole stupid conversation. We were clearly annoying her almost beyond endurance.

"How would we get permission?" he asked.

"Oh," she scoffed, "that would be at the Ministry. Anyhow, permission would have to be given personally by the Minister himself, and that cannot happen."

"Where would that Ministry be?" Ken asked calmly, like it was the most natural question in the world.

"In Potsdam!" she shouted triumphantly, certain it would finally end the conversation.

"Could you let us have the address, please?" Ken asked firmly.

"You are not allowed to go there. It is seventy kilometres away and they close at four o'clock, so it will be a complete waste of time anyway."

Then, as we sat there determined and resolute, Frau Steglitz paused for a second, as if weighing up in her mind whether giving us an address was likely to be to her advantage; perhaps by getting three troublesome foreigners out of her office she could pass us on for someone else to deal with. Whatever it was, something seemed to occur to her and without a word she stood up and strode from the room. Ken and I exchanged glances but dared not say a word. There was a terrible tension in the air. Had she gone to fetch the guards to have us dealt with? The minutes ticked by as we waited, not knowing what fate now lay in store for us. Ken glanced at his watch but said nothing. It was already two o'clock. It was surprising how the hours would ebb away when you were constantly waiting for permissions to do things.

To our astonishment she returned five minutes later with an address typed on a very small sheet of paper. We curtly nodded our thanks and shook her hand, behaving as if we considered she had done no more than her duty. Frau Steglitz escorted us out of the building and we left quickly. I could hardly believe our luck. I was overcome with relief. We had taken a decisive step forward.

"Next stop Potsdam, then," I announced as we climbed back into the car.

Ken was working it out. "Potsdam is 70 kilometres in the opposite direction from Checkpoint Charlie. Even if we manage to get there before the Ministry closes there's a real chance we wouldn't make it back in time to meet our deadline."

But this was such a huge breakthrough I couldn't bear the thought of turning round and going home, risking that we would not be allowed back in again another day. We didn't have permission from anyone to go there, but then the chances were that we wouldn't be given permission to come back again either. It seemed like a risk we simply had to take. Taking them by surprise seemed to be working to our advantage so far.

"We've got to get there as quickly as possible," I said before Ken could protest any more about how dangerous it was. "Let's make a dash for it."

80

He stared at me for a few seconds and then turned to Anthony.

"OK," he said grimly. "Let's go to Potsdam."

CHAPTER
EIGHT

Charming the Minister

Anthony was very quiet as he drove, concentrating on avoiding the rusty little Trabant cars which veered past us in the opposite direction as their drivers stared open-mouthed at the strange sight of a sleek, western Mercedes in their midst. I began to think about Emilie and pulled her little portrait out of my handbag. Giving it a fleeting glance I renewed my promise, that I would find her wherever the past had hidden her, before tucking the portrait away again. We were all looking around for police patrols, afraid that if we were held up now it would surely be the end of our adventure. We were aware that Anthony was exceeding the speed limits, but the thought of missing our chance of catching the ministry and of being late back for our deadline at Checkpoint Charlie was more frightening than the thought of being stopped for speeding.

"What's that noise?" I asked when we were about halfway to our destination, picking up a growing droning noise. "It's right above us. What is it?"

"It's a helicopter," Anthony said, glancing in the mirror, his lips tight. "It's been following us for the last few miles but I didn't want to say anything. I was hoping it would go away."

"Just keep going," I said before either of the others could protest. "If they were going to stop us they would have done it by now."

"They're just keeping an eye on us to make sure we don't go anywhere we shouldn't," Ken agreed.

The helicopter tracked us for another ten minutes or so before peeling away. Maybe it had decided we were now someone else's problem. We drove into the built-up outskirts of Potsdam nearly an hour later. Potsdam had once been a famous city; a former residence of Prussian kings, containing fabulous royal palaces built during the reign of Frederick the Great and situated on beautiful lakes. It had also been a centre for scientific research. To our eyes that day, however, it looked more like a battle zone. It didn't seem like any of the buildings had been repaired or even given a lick of paint since the end of the war. The walls were still pockmarked with bullet holes and there were bomb craters and piles of sandbags everywhere we looked. All the scarred and shabby buildings were coated in what looked like centuries of coal dust. As we drew close to what we hoped was the address on the piece of paper we slowed down and three enormous soldiers bearing Kalashnikov rifles appeared from nowhere and headed towards us, shouting orders, forcing us to pull up sharply.

"*Vyhodite iz mashiny pozhaluista!*"

"Oh my God," Ken muttered, "we've crossed over into the Russian sector."

The lead soldier gestured with his gun for Ken to get out of the car before snapping out another order.

"Documents?" Ken asked, reaching gingerly into his pocket for our passports, "yes, yes."

Anthony and I waited in the car, watching anxiously as Ken tried to explain what we wanted to the soldiers. We saw him showing them the scrap of paper we had been given by Frau Steglitz and one of them pointing towards a nearby building.

"I won't be a minute," Ken called back to us as he walked away.

"Where are you going?" I shouted, alarmed at the thought of our being separated, frightened that by being so impetuous I had put all our lives in danger. What if he disappeared into the building and never emerged again? What would we do then? I wanted to go with him, even though he had ordered me to stay in the car, but he was already climbing the steps in front of the building the soldier had directed him to.

Inside, I found out later, he nearly fell straight into another uncovered bomb crater. The whole area was wrecked. Recovering himself and adjusting his eyes to the gloom, he managed to find an East German soldier he could communicate with. He showed the man the typed address with the same authoritative flourish he had used when producing the fictitious invitation letter.

Anthony and I both breathed a sigh of relief as we saw the two of them emerging back through the door and Ken waved for us to get out of the car and come with them, our every move followed by the suspicious eyes of the Russian guards. The soldier led us a few yards down the street and another official poked his head out of a cubbyhole in the side of the building as we approached.

"What is your business here?" he demanded angrily.

"We have come to see someone about permission to study at the Merseburg Archives," Ken said, presenting our passports yet again. No one listening to his firm tone of voice would have guessed how anxious he actually was. We had stepped through a door back into the fearful darkness of Europe in the 1940s and knew that we would be at mercy of the Russians should they discover we were not even allowed to be there.

The man in the cubbyhole seemed used to being ordered around and scuttled away with the passports, leaving us under the watchful stare of the guard with no idea what was going to happen to us next. He returned a few minutes later but it was impossible to tell from his expression what reaction to our arrival he had received.

"The Minister will see you now," he said.

Ken and I exchanged disbelieving looks. We were shocked. Had we really managed to reach the heart of the government in just one day? We hardly dared to accept what was happening. Things were moving so fast it was unnerving. If Frau Steglitz had been scary, I wondered, what was this man going to be like? We followed our guide up a flight of stairs with a quickening pace. I wondered if the Ministry was about to close since it was now nearly four o'clock.

"Please," the man said, stopping outside an imposing door, "enter."

Ken allowed me to go through first and I stepped cautiously round the corner and straight into another world. I was instantly dazzled by the splendour of the room and didn't notice the man inside until he spoke.

"Welcome to you," a friendly voice greeted us. "Please come in and make yourselves comfortable." This was not what I had expected at all.

The Minister was standing next to a great, handsome mahogany desk, which sat in front of a window overlooking a tranquil courtyard garden glowing with the colours of its spring flowers. The atmosphere was calm and the room was warm and welcoming. The Minister's swept-back black hair glistened with Brylcreem and he beamed as he shook our hands with exaggerated courtesy and invited us to sit down and relax in the splendour of his office.

"What can I do for you?" he enquired, walking back to his chair and sitting down.

It was quite possibly the first smile we had seen since leaving West Berlin and we probably responded with grateful expressions, despite our puzzlement at the effusiveness of the welcome.

"So," he beamed, directing his gaze at me, "do tell me, why have you come here, Mrs Haas?"

"I have written a letter to the archive in Merseburg to ask for their permission to look for my great, great grandmother," I explained. "She lived with the Prince August of Prussia for many years."

"Have you had a reply to your letter?" he asked.

"No."

"I fear you never will," he beamed apologetically. He seemed to be saying that he understood completely and shared my frustration, but what could be done in the face of such an inflexible system? "They have been very naughty. Your letter should have been handed to me to deal with, but instead it ended up there." He pointed to his wastepaper basket. At that moment East-West politics meant nothing. It was as if we were both allies in our shared lost cause, two human beings engaging in conversation for no other reason than we seemed to like each other. My guard went down under the full glare of his charm.

"Mr Haas, please will you write down details of your request for me," the Minister said and Ken proceeded to write down the details as he was asked.

"Your courtyard is absolutely delightful," I told him.

He turned to the garden, following my gaze through the window. "Spring is such a lovely time of year, isn't it?"

Most of the people we had come across so far had concentrated all their attention on Ken rather than me. He was, after all, the senior member of our mission because of his age and gender. But now the Minister's eyes were locked onto me so fiercely it was as if there were no one else in the room. His attentiveness and courtly politeness quite knocked the stuffing out of me. I had been preparing myself to be met by more suspicion and aggression and I was not expecting to come across flirtation instead. I felt a surge of relief to be with someone who acted like he was our supporter.

It seemed like nothing was going to be too much trouble for this man.

"So, let me get this straight," he said, leaning forward and furrowing his brow to show just how hard he was concentrating on what I was saying. "You came here all the way from England, through all our border controls, deep into the heart of our country, in order to find your great, great grandmother?"

"Yes, I did," I said. "That is why I am here."

"Incredible. Are you a gardener?" he asked, seeing my eyes flicker once again to the scene outside the window.

"Um, well yes," I said, a little startled by the sudden change of subject.

He leaned closer towards me, talking to me and ignoring Ken and Anthony completely. They might as well not have been in the room. The Minister's eyes were fixed on mine. I tried to ignore Ken's growing irritation and then, just as suddenly, the Minister changed the subject back again.

"I will help you find your great, great grandmother, Mrs Haas. Please let me have the paper, Mr Haas. In ten days' time you will receive an official permission to study in our archives. You can be certain of it."

This man had access to the secrets of my family's past, perhaps he even held the key to what really happened more than a century ago. I still couldn't hope to know whether I would ever find Emilie and learn about her life with August, but as we walked out of the Minister's office there was a spring in my step because

I felt sure now that Emilie's spirit truly was willing me on.

A few minutes later we were back outside in the real world, in the grimy, run-down street, picking our way through the potholes and past the Russian soldiers to the waiting car. Had it been a dream? Did it really happen? It didn't seem possible that the Minister's little oasis was no more than a few metres away, safely hidden behind these shabby walls.

"Don't think just because he made eyes at you that you will actually receive the permission from him," Ken muttered as the three of us hurried back to the car. And just as I was thinking I had detected a hint of jealousy in his voice, he added, "don't believe a word of it."

I pretended to agree, not wanting to seem that I was gullible or had been flattered by the Minister's attentions, but actually I had to believe it because if I didn't then my search would be at an end. I knew that without the Minister's permission, gaining access to the files that held all the secrets I was so desperately looking for would remain a distant dream. Although I kept quiet in the car as we sped back towards the border, not wanting to seem naïve, I was secretly bubbling with optimism. I couldn't believe how much we had managed to achieve in just one day and I didn't want anything to bring my mood down. It had gone so well we had over an hour to spare before our eight o'clock deadline as Checkpoint Charlie came into sight and I heaved a sigh of relief. I was hankering for the comfort of our hotel room in West Berlin and the idea of dropping into a warm bath and tucking into a well-earned dinner was now uppermost on my mind.

"They're waving me to pull over," Anthony said as we got closer to the East German guards, and I felt my heart sink again. "They want us to get out."

We were no longer in the warm, welcoming office of a Minister, we were now standing beside a bleak piece of road having questions fired at us by unsmiling and suspicious soldiers who didn't seem remotely impressed by our passports or any letters we might have. They questioned us minutely about everything we had done that day and everyone we had seen. If they were impressed by the Minister's name they didn't show it with even a flicker of their stony expressions. They behaved like they wanted to ensure that we didn't think we were anyone special just because we were driving out of their country in a nice car, having spent the day talking to important people. They certainly wanted to remind us that they were the ones in charge, not us. They were, after all, the ones with the guns and the authority to arrest us should they so decide.

Eventually they could think of no more reasons to delay our departure and they nodded us through without even a flash of eye contact. As far as they were concerned we were beneath their contempt. By then we didn't care what they thought of us, just as long as we were safely back in the West. The moment we drew up at the next barrier we asked the soldiers to inform the British Consul that we had returned. It had been an incredible day, but would we ever be allowed to get any further in our search for the truth?

CHAPTER
NINE

The Disappearing Passports

All I thought about back in London over the next ten days was whether the Minister would keep his word or whether, as Ken was convinced, I had been bamboozled by his charm and easily made promises. My moods swung wildly between optimism and pessimism. One moment I would be reminding myself how well we had got on in our search so far and seeing no reason why our luck shouldn't continue to hold; the next moment I would be trying to see any reason at all why the Minister or Frau Steglitz or anyone else in the East would bother to give us a second thought once we had left their offices. Despite getting inside the castle walls of the archive, and despite all the Minister's glibly delivered promises, we had still not found out anything about August or Emilie, which was frustrating. But I simply had to keep the faith. He had promised me we would hear in ten days and as that deadline crept ever closer, the tension inside my head was becoming unbearable.

Each morning and afternoon the postman brought us no news and by the start of the tenth day I could hardly contain my sense of anticipation. My disappointment when there was yet again no envelope from East Germany to be found on the doormat that morning was hard to bear. Ken, never one to crow when he was proved right and knowing how sad I was about being let down, said nothing and I tried to put on a brave face. And then in the second post on that tenth day a poor-quality envelope bearing East German stamps flopped through the letterbox onto the hall floor. I could hardly breathe as I opened it and I had to read the words several times before I could be sure I had understood them correctly.

"What does it say, Mum?" our second son, Timothy wanted to know. Of all three of the boys he had become the most infected by my enthusiasm and was almost as anxious as I was to find out the truth about our ancestors.

"I can't believe it," I said, reading it through yet again, clamping my hand firmly across my mouth to stop myself shouting for joy.

"What does it say?" He could barely hold back his excitement.

"He has given us unlimited access to the archives. He has given permission for us to stay in East Germany for as long as we need to in order to complete the research. We can travel wherever we want to."

I rushed through to tell Ken, who obviously assumed I had misunderstood the letter and immediately took it from me to read himself.

"This is great news," he said with a gulp. "Well done. It seems I misjudged the man after all."

I knew that Ken still had many reservations and I appreciated how hard it was for him to accept that we would have to spend more time behind the Iron Curtain if we were to have any chance at all of finding Emilie. It was now even harder for him to swallow this prospect given that the Minister's letter had exceeded even my expectations. We were being given permission to stay in East Germany for as long as we liked, and presumably by that the Minister meant until I found what I was looking for, my great, great grandmother, Emilie Gottschalk. Ken was clearly very worried after settling down to the idea and once he had had more time to think about all the ramifications of the Minister's letter. He knew full well that I wanted to take advantage of every little morsel of opportunity I was offered, following up any opening that might help me to reach my goal.

For my part I had made up my mind that no stone would be left unturned, and I had already demonstrated that my resolve was sincere. The Minister was giving us everything I had asked for, but what would Frau Steglitz be thinking, I wondered, when she discovered the result of our forbidden foray into Potsdam, after we had so relentlessly pushed her into giving us the address? I felt buoyed up because, despite all the grave advice she and others had handed out to me, my dogged determination and stubbornness had borne fruit so spectacularly. Yet again I found myself wondering if any of our good luck could be Emilie's doing?

I knew Ken was doing the whole thing for me, and by not trying to talk me out of it any more he was showing me just how courageous he was. I understood that I was asking a lot of him but the urge to find out about my family's hidden past had become overpowering. The verbal legacy I had inherited was driving me on and I truly thought that he would agree with me that it had all been worth it once we had achieved our objective and returned home safely. I set about making the preparations to return to Merseburg.

A week later Ken and I were crossing the border at Checkpoint Charlie once more, armed with our golden letter from the Minister and this time without Anthony as our chaperone. In an attempt to ease Ken's fears I had agreed to stay for just a week and had promised him that if we hadn't found my great, great grandparents in that time I would still return to the West with him without making any sort of fuss. I was feeling so optimistic at that stage that I was sure a week would be enough for the secrets of the archives to be revealed to us.

The British Consul in West Berlin had been as amazed by our success with the Minister as Ken and I had been. When even the archivist in Dahlem had been so defensive and uncooperative it was hard to imagine why the authorities in the East were suddenly opening their arms to us when they had never agreed to such a thing before, even for distinguished professors of history. I was just grateful and excited that they had agreed and eager to the point of impatience to start work.

Even with the Minister's letter in Ken's pocket, however, our experiences with the surly border guards on our way out the time before meant we still expected that the bureaucrats and functionaries lower down the chain of command were likely to continue to give us a hard time. Our assumptions proved correct. The guards at the border were just as suspicious and aggressive as they had been before. Eventually, however, they had no choice but to let us pass.

As soon as we walked through the doors of our hotel in Halle we were hit by the Spartan and gloomy atmosphere of the place, which was built in the typically featureless communist style. Halle was a town conveniently situated around twenty minutes' drive away from the Merseburg Archive. We were greeted by a receptionist hardly less demanding than the border guards had just been. She insisted that we handed over our passports to her as soon as we appeared, practically snatching them out of our hands before immediately disappearing into another room with them.

We stood waiting for a while, expecting them to be returned once the details had been checked, but nothing happened for twenty minutes. Uncomfortable at suddenly being behind the Iron Curtain without any identification papers, Ken decided to try pulling some rank and waved the Minister's letter at another receptionist. The letter was snatched from his hand and followed the passports through a door and into oblivion.

Eventually the first receptionist returned and we asked if we could have the passports back now.

"We need to keep your passports," she said, seeming surprised to find us still standing there. "They are going to the police."

"But we have all the necessary permissions from the Minister to be here," I protested. "We need to have our papers for identification. Why can't we have them back? What is the problem?"

"You must stay inside the hotel," she said, ignoring my questions. "When the passports are returned, then you can go outside. Not before."

We tried pleading but she seemed not to be able to hear us any more. It was like we were invisible and inaudible as she went back to her paperwork, as if to indicate that our conversation with her was over. Nothing we could say would make any difference. Our instructions were clear, even if the reasons for them were not. We were restricted to staying within the walls of that depressing hotel until we were told we could leave and we had no way of getting in touch with our friend, the Minister, in order to appeal for help. The thought of going outside and being stopped by the police, without having any papers to show who we were, was even less attractive than remaining imprisoned in the hotel. In fact, we might as well have been arrested for all the freedom we now had. Without our passports we couldn't even return to the West to wait in comfort while things were sorted out by the police. I could tell that this was fuelling all of Ken's worst fears, but he didn't say anything; that was the kind of person he was.

I was desperate to get to work in the archives but there was nothing to do but sit around the hotel room and wait, having no idea what was going on behind the scenes and watching the hours tick away, eating into my precious week. The waiting did nothing to calm Ken's discomfort at being virtual prisoners in a totalitarian country. Was anyone actually looking into our case or had the passports merely been tossed onto a pile on someone's desk along with a hundred other pending jobs? There was no way for us to know. If that was the case, how long would it be before our turn came round and our passports reached the top of the pile?

So much of my time during that period seemed to be spent in limbo, waiting for someone else to do something but not knowing if they ever would. Being at someone else's mercy was not a comfortable place to be.

The rest of our first day dragged past impossibly slowly. Every time we went to the reception desk to enquire how much longer it would be, they shrugged and went back to whatever they were doing without bothering to answer. It was of no consequence to them how angry we might become. The afternoon came and went and we were forced to eat a tasteless supper and go to bed without having any idea if we would be able to get started on our quest the next morning or whether we would be left sitting in the hotel again.

The following day was exactly the same. It was like living in a terrible grey vacuum with no distractions from the frustration and boredom. With nothing else to do we spent endless hours watching whatever was happening in the hotel, which wasn't much. There was a fresh-faced young boy working as a waiter in the dining room and I found myself speculating on what his life must be like in such an oppressive, humourless world. He told us his name was Victor and seemed pleased to have someone different to talk to. We told him a little of our problem.

"Frustrating, isn't it?" he said. "Be grateful you don't live here. Do you want to hear a joke?"

"You're allowed jokes in this country?" Ken asked.

"Of course," he grinned mischievously, "forbidden ones like this one. A Russian man is queuing for bread. The queue stretches for miles. He turns to his friend and says, 'I can't stand this any more. I'm going off to kill President Brezhnev!' And he walks away in anger. A while later he comes back. 'What happened?' asks the friend. 'Arghh, the queue to kill Brezhnev was even longer,' he says."

As he finished the joke we both laughed and then noticed that the manager was looking disapprovingly in our direction. Laughter was unusual in that hotel and apparently not encouraged. Victor saw the look on his boss's face too and realised he had overstepped the mark. He hurried away, muttering about an important job that needed doing.

On the third day of having nothing to do we decided that we no longer had anything to lose by making a fuss. If we didn't do something we were in danger of losing our minds and we might end up reaching the end of the week without ever having stepped out of the hotel. Taking deep breaths we marched together to reception as a united front. The girl looked up at us with the usual expressionless eyes and held out two passports and the Minister's letter.

"Here are your passports," she said. "You may now leave the hotel. We are sorry for the delay."

We were so relieved that our gratitude for this small favour was almost pathetic, and she shot us a contemptuous look before very deliberately going back to her work, as if to let us know we had been dismissed. We hurried away, anxious both to get to work and to avoid annoying her any further. It doesn't take long for any authoritarian regime to break a person's spirit if they are determined enough to do so. We walked straight out to the car and set out for the archives, preparing ourselves to do battle next with the terrifying Frau Steglitz.

"Be very careful, Evi," Ken warned as we approached the castle. "Remember, we need to have this woman on our side if we want to be shown anything at all. If she decides to deny that there are any files on Prince August it will be impossible for us to prove otherwise."

I knew he was right. If she told us there was nothing in the files for us to see then we would be left once again staring at the walls with nothing to do for the rest of the week. We had to find a way of involving her in the excitement of the hunt, so that she became as enthused by the chase for the truth as we were.

Frau Steglitz came out immediately to greet us when she heard that we had arrived. Amazingly the gorgon we had met on our previous visit had been replaced by an entirely different woman. Her face wreathed in smiles, she seemed genuinely pleased and excited to see us again. All the aggression and defensiveness had vanished. Was it the Minister's letter? Had it given her permission to become a human being and to actually enjoy her job? Presumably she had become an archivist in the first place because she was interested in history and in research, and we were offering her a wonderful opportunity to indulge herself in both. It seemed like our luck had returned to us along with our passports, at least for a while.

"I hope you are enjoying your stay with us?" she beamed, sounding so genuinely concerned that we didn't have the heart to tell her what a living hell the previous three days of boredom and uncertainty had been. "Now, I would like to introduce you to our archivist, Herr Waltmann. He will be looking after you while you are studying with us."

She showed us into a spacious, sparsely furnished reading room with well-worn wooden floors and tables. The most noticeable thing about it was the deadly silence that hung in the air. A couple of other people were already leafing soundlessly through piles of documents, but they didn't even look up from their studies as we came in. Frau Steglitz settled us down at a round desk in a sectioned-off area before going off to find Herr Waltmann. I suddenly felt nervous again, but for different reasons this time. After all this effort, what if there still proved to be nothing to find? What if it had all just been a stupid fantasy and my father had been right all along? I wasn't sure how I would cope with the disappointment if that turned out to be the case. But, I told myself, there was nothing I could do about that now; I had set my course and I must just sail ahead and hope for the best.

CHAPTER
TEN

The Opening of the Archives

Herr Waltmann was neatly dressed and in his forties. Immaculately polite, he seemed genuinely interested to meet us, although a little reserved, which I could understand given his position and situation. It was becoming increasingly obvious to me that anyone who dealt with Westerners had to be careful not to be accused of being too friendly. Nevertheless, Herr Waltmann was preparing us adequately to receive whatever he could find that might shed light on the period in history relevant to the lives of my ancestors. Most of them had been residents of my own former home city, Berlin, which had been my whole life until 1934; the year Hitler murdered his way to power. Here we were now, back in the East, 31 years after the allies had defeated the man whose monstrous evil had all but destroyed Western Europe. How perverse it was for me to be back in a part of my mother country that was now occupied and governed by another dictatorship. This time it was a communist one, with all its punitive restrictions and daily threats to its citizens, keeping them in check and maintaining an iron and undemocratic grip on power.

I understood that we couldn't expect the process that we had set off to be an instant one, and for files and documents to be made immediately accessible to us. We could only hope for the best, putting ourselves in the hands of Herr Waltmann. He was a nice enough man but Ken brought me back into the real world when he whispered, "We will only be seeing whatever they allow us to see."

We were still at the mercy of a totalitarian regime but, whatever might be going on behind closed doors, I was prepared to wait for however long it would take to uncover the evidence that I needed. Whether it would be minutes or hours, it didn't matter to me. I was used to waiting and this was the last place on earth, it seemed to me, that could hold the answers to all the questions that had been taunting me for so long and pervading all my thoughts. I was sure that with Ken on my side we would stay put until my task was complete.

About twenty minutes later Herr Waltmann reappeared in the reading room. He was bearing a pile of bulky files, which all looked ancient and shabby. Instead of placing the heavy load on the desk before us, as I was expecting, he stood there for a moment.

He then announced with obvious relish. "You are the first people to see these papers. Nobody has seen these files in one hundred and thirty years."

With that he placed his load reverently down onto the desk and, stepping back, he lifted his arm and gestured proudly to the dusty pile.

"They belonged to the King of Prussia and his family, the Hohenzollern, the rulers of the Prussian Kingdom, before the formation of Germany."

"What are they all about?" I asked, a little daunted by the size of the pile, knowing that if I kept my word to Ken, we now only had four days left to study them. Even from a cursory glance I could see that much of the language was archaic and difficult and the writing dense and hard to decipher. Each page would take a lot of time to study if we hoped to find every clue that might be hidden within the closely packed lines.

"Here you will find the life of our Prince August of Prussia," Herr Waltmann said.

In those few words he had thrown the world at my feet. My Prince August, my great, great grandfather was lying on the table in front of me. Whatever was I going to find out now? These documents had been seen by nobody in over a century. My father had said there was nothing to find, that nothing existed, but it looked like he was wrong about August. Would he be wrong about Emilie and the family connection as well? I was hell-bent on finding out.

"Why on earth has nobody seen them in one hundred and thirty years," I asked Ken, for some reason expecting him to be able to give me an answer, putting everything right in an instant and solving the mystery. I always had such confidence in his wisdom.

"How should I know, Eve?" came the reply I should have expected.

With a courteous little bow Herr Waltmann backed out of the room, leaving us with the files. With bated breath I gingerly picked up the top ones. There was no doubting how old they were and some of them were in such poor condition, crisp and yellow with age, that I was frightened they were going to crumble to dust in my hands. Tense with excitement I started to turn over the pages on the top of the pile, almost immediately jumping back with surprise.

"Diaries and notes written in August's own hand, Ken," I exclaimed, hardly able to contain myself. There in front of me was the handwriting of August, just like it was in the front of the notebook, telling me so many details about his life.

Ken's knowledge of old German was far more exacting than mine. Thankfully my father had insisted that we carried on speaking German at home all those years ago, which had meant I never lost my mother tongue and could still speak German fluently. Even so, I felt more secure in Ken's hands when it came to the more difficult Gothic German. I waited impatiently for him to tell me what he was discovering.

"These are meticulously maintained," he said, admiringly. "August talks about his private and his military life."

Ken thumbed further through the pile.

"There are letters, household accounts for his palaces and historical and military records," he enthused.

I was thrilled to see so much material existed, and there was more to come. I could see that the quantity of it all meant that we were never going to get through all these records in the few days we had left but I couldn't bring myself to even think of asking Ken to extend our stay after all the promises I had made to him.

To have got this far was an amazing achievement. I was staring at files that had been hidden away for 130 years. Was I about to finally prove my father wrong? What was I going to find out about August? Would my journey back to the 1800s reveal anything about my family or about why they, and Prince August, had been so effectively expunged from historical records? Taking a deep breath I pulled my thoughts back under control and started turning the pages.

"It's mostly in Gothic German, not just his diaries," I said quietly, not wanting to disturb any of our neighbours at the other tables for fear of being thrown back out on the street before I had even started my quest. "This is not going to be easy."

"Heads down then," Ken said and we both set about reading.

CHAPTER
ELEVEN

My Great, Great Grandfather – Prince August of Prussia

As the hours ticked silently by and we grew more used to both the writing and the old-fashioned use of language, we became absorbed in the words that were crammed into every page, transported back to a time when Napoleon had elevated himself to the position of Emperor of France and King of the Italians. As I sifted through the documents I realised the enormity of what was happening to me.

Prince August was not just my own flesh and blood, and a royal prince who met and fell in love with a Jewish girl, the reason why we were here. My Prince August was also turning out to be the defender of the realm against Napoleon as the "little emperor" rampaged across Europe, causing havoc and threatening all the monarchies. It was a startling discovery.

The Hohenzollern monarchs ruled the Prussian Empire, the capital of a whole group of states that were

107

eventually to become Germany. The mighty European empires of the day were the Prussians, the Austrians, the English and the Russians, and war seemed to be the natural and constant threat between all of them. There was so much information to absorb and understand it was hard to know where to start.

Every so often one of the archive staff would kindly bring us a hot drink, or one or other of us would have to visit the washroom, but there were no other distractions. We became so absorbed we didn't even think to eat until we arrived back at the hotel that evening, exhausted and excited by our discoveries, itching to get back and find out more.

The first day seemed to merge into the second, with very little sleep during the night as my head constantly throbbed with the excitement of what I had discovered. When we rolled back into the archive as it opened the next morning I quickly returned to evaluating the man who I believed would be Emilie's partner twenty-five years hence. Would August be suitable for her? He was certainly eligible. I pictured what he would have looked like. I hoped that he was the dashing, handsome prince that I had been dreaming about. It felt as though I was embarking on a courtship myself, albeit a most unusual one.

The papers we had been given were taking us into his life during the battles with Napoleon. The family appeared to be grooming the young August, bringing him up and training him to be a soldier and a leader. He was already a major by the time he reached 21. The achievements of Prussia under Frederick the Great,

August's uncle, had earned it a fearsome reputation. Well defended, its military superiority allowed it at least some respite from the struggles that were going on around it, but that would not last for long. The family myth had led me to this mighty prince, who by 1804 was already commanding a battalion of grenadiers.

The Prussian king, Frederick William III, had to make a decision about Napoleon. Uncertain what to do with such a determined enemy he was trying for appeasement and the young August was lobbying heavily for the Prussians to stand up to Napoleon before it was too late. There were documents in the files that were loaded with famous signatures backing up August's case to the King for fighting rather than appeasing. Suddenly I found myself there, right back in my Berlin as it stood under threat. I was willing August on, fearing for his safety. He was absorbing me completely. The French had grown enormously in strength and August was telling everyone that if the Prussians didn't strike quickly they could soon be overwhelmed by this newly superior force. Even the Queen, who was an influential figure, believed that the never-ending balls and festivities of the Prussian Court should cease forthwith. The very survival of the Prussian State was at stake and the Empire needed to take up arms to protect itself.

"Look at this," I hissed to Ken, sliding a document across to him. It showed that August and his elder brother, Louis Ferdinand, had had enough of the King's shilly-shallying. They'd gone to meet him in Breslau in East Prussia, the city where I was born no less! "They are presenting him with a petition, an ultimatum, forcing him to fight Napoleon, can you believe it?"

I wondered how much Emilie knew about all of this history when she met August. Was she seduced by his power and his courage in the way that I was being seduced as I read about it? By the time they met he had already lived a full and colourful life, the same life that I was entering now. How would that have made her feel? Would she have been as consumed as I was? As I read I kept hoping for a clue as to what might lie in the future for the Prince, but there was nothing in these papers that helped me, or dropped any hints that would lead me to what I was looking for — Emilie Gottschalk.

It was still only 1805. The Tsar of Russia was finally persuading the King of Prussia to join the Austro-Russian Alliance against France and the Prussian army was being mobilised. I was on the front line, witnessing a first-hand account of the events that I knew from all the history lessons of my childhood would shape Europe for the next hundred years. The alliance against Napoleon was sealed with a ceremonial handshake beside the grave of Frederick the Great, and Prince August had finally got his wish. The following pages and handwritten diary excerpts took us back into the heat of the battles that were raging. Even though there was still no sign of Emilie I was intoxicated by this vivid account of huge historical events that was unravelling before my very own eyes.

I had to pinch myself to remember that Prince August wasn't just a great historical figure, but that he was the future partner of Emilie, my great, great grandmother. I wanted to know more personal details about him. Was he honourable? Was he a ladies' man who stole hearts and then broke them? There were so many unanswered questions. If he was so powerful how was it possible that he could just disappear from history without leaving a trace? And what happened to Charlotte, the daughter that we believed Emilie had borne him? My father and Uncle Freddy had both been certain that he and Emilie spent the last eleven years of his life happily together, but where was the proof? Where was the documentation?

I feared the worst as I read about Louis Ferdinand, August's glamorous and famously extravagant older brother. He was marching towards the battlefield at Saalfield to confront the French on his white charger, Slop. I felt that I was hearing the news as it was happening. Ken glanced up, concerned by the look on my face.

"What's up?" he enquired as my hand covered my mouth. Louis Ferdinand had been struck down in battle.

"Napoleon has killed Louis Ferdinand," I exclaimed, louder than I meant to, making other heads rise up from their studies around the room and someone to shush me.

"What year?" Ken whispered back.

"1806."

"So," he said, doing a quick calculation in his head, "August would have been 27 years old when his brother died."

He was reading and translating with me now, equally excited. The death of such a famous and revered soldier had had a terrible effect on the morale of the entire Prussian army. It seemed like a fearful precursor of what might happen next. There were reports of how the news had moved the whole army to tears.

"Good God! They brought Slop to August with his brother's blood still on the saddle," Ken said. "Look at this: August is giving a rousing speech to the troops about the destiny of Prussia lying in his hands. He's climbed back into Slop's saddle and has set off into battle to avenge his brother death. August is rousing his troops before he leads them into battle, 'Today, I also have another sacred duty to fulfil, to avenge my brother who died gloriously for our beloved Fatherland. Grenadiers and artillerists, swear to me that you will always follow me and be assured that I shall always lead you along the path of honour and glory.' "

As I listened to Ken translating in a hoarse whisper, nervous of disturbing the other readers, I was right by August's side, taking on his struggles against Napoleon. I could hear the cheers of the soldiers, all of them inspired to have a leader who was willing to risk his life alongside them. I imagined how resplendent he would have looked in his shako, bearing Prussian eagles and gold chains that shone like the polished buttons on his dark blue coat. What an awesome sight — August was holding his gleaming sabre up above his head as he galloped into battle on his dead brother's great white charger, hungry for revenge and victory.

Then there was the terrifying picture, the horror of the battlefields. I was witnessing it all, as August led from the front in yet another charge, with dead bodies lying all around and the smell of smoke and gunpowder hanging in the air. My ancestor was ready to die for Prussia; he was a brave fighter indeed. He truly had made a difference to history and I felt proud and deeply moved.

But victory was not yet within August's grasp. The Prussian army was being led by the Duke of Brunswick. Disaster struck when the Duke was shot in the head during the battle of Jena-Auerstedt a few days after the death of Louis Ferdinand, leaving him blinded and unconscious. The Duke later died of his wounds. Ken and I had come to Merseburg to discover Emilie, that was the only reason why we were there, yet now I found myself in the middle of a bitter war with Napoleon, embedded in hand-to-hand fighting, hoping against hope that my great, great grandfather would success-fully beat off the aggressor whose relentless onslaught on Prussia was costing countless numbers of lives. The King was not competent to take over the leadership of the troops and so the courageous Prussian generals battled on for as long as they could on their own, until eventually the might of the French proved too much for them and they were driven back. August managed to rally his grenadiers for one last charge, covering the retreating soldiers, but was unable to rally them for a return to battle. It was a mighty and gallant effort. At the mercy of these horrendous conditions, August was finally defeated in the mud and the chaos at Prenzlau. When the news of the defeat reached the royal family the Queen immediately packed up and fled Berlin, further undermining the confidence of the Prussian people. It was beginning to look as if the previously all-powerful Prussian Empire of Frederick the Great had finally met its match.

August's account was as gripping as in any movie. In the end, despite his ferocity and determination, he was captured, and very lucky not to have been killed in the battle. The victors immediately robbed August of his Order of the Black Eagle and his pocket watch. Both of which were returned to him once his captors realised who he was, although they still insisted that he paid them to return Slop, who was running around in a blind, riderless panic in the marshlands where the Prince's battalion had finally become bogged down.

Very soon the King had fled the country and Napoleon was sitting in Frederick the Great's magnificent Charlottenburg Palace in Berlin, having marched triumphantly through the Brandenburg Gate. The descriptions painted a vivid picture of just how violent and bloody hand-to-hand warfare was in those days. To thrive in such a ferocious and frightening arena, Prince August had to have been a man of massive physical strength as well as courage. His capture was a massive coup for Napoleon.

This most valuable prisoner, caked in mud and dishevelled, was brought before Napoleon. With one boot missing, having been left behind stuck in the muddy marshes, a defiant Prince August stood face to face with his arch-enemy, who had been waiting for him in Frederick the Great's rooms. The victor and the vanquished squared up to one another — what a sight that must have been, the tall Prussian and diminutive Corsican. August stubbornly refused to answer any questions put to him. Despite whatever he might feel about the Prussian Prince as an enemy, Napoleon later professed himself greatly impressed with the dignity and fearsome loyalty that August showed in that moment of defeat. Realising that the Prince was an immensely popular figure, the French Emperor decided to spare his life, putting him under house arrest in Berlin instead. Napoleon had already been to visit August's parents at the Bellevue Palace, since August's father was known to be still strongly in favour of an alliance between France and Prussia. Napoleon was willing to allow August to return to the family home as long as he kept the night-time curfew imposed on him.

August, however, was not so easily controlled and would steal out at night to rally his men and raise an army. Napoleon found out and on Christmas night August was woken roughly by French officers who spirited him out of Prussia, his destination the castle prison of Nancy in France. Uhde, his faithful secretary, and his adjutant, Clausewitz, were taken with him. August requested that his mother be informed of what was happening and she was awakened to see the distressing sight of her son being escorted from the palace.

Napoleon accused August of plotting against him with other Prussian officers; yet again he was still prepared to spare his life. I was later to find out the depth of Napoleon's respect for this strong-willed young Prussian soldier who was not prepared to sit quietly for long when his beloved country was under occupation by an enemy force.

I was beginning to wonder how Ken and I would ever be able to get through all the notes and documents that were now stacked in front of us in the time we had left, but I was loathe to skip through any of the densely written texts in case I missed some vital fact or admission.

Eventually, as peace became a possibility, Napoleon allowed August to socialise freely and the young ladies of Nancy flocked to meet the handsome and dashing young Prince. Nancy became a life of balls and parties and the Prince danced the nights away, much to the disapproval of his friend and adjutant, the sober Clausewitz. August was just as interested in helping some of the other 5000 Prussian prisoners of war in the town who were not enjoying the same freedoms as him. He tried to ensure that they were fed and treated fairly, while at the same time secretly preparing them for the moment when they would be able to regroup and become an army once more. The suspicious Emperor, however, got wind of his plans and ordered that he be moved once more to another castle at Soissons. Being a prince made imprisonment a very different experience and August and Clausewitz still had the freedom to work together a great deal, drawing up a plan for reforming the Prussian army once a peace deal with France could finally be worked out.

On their release in 1807, after the signing of the Paris Peace Treaty, while August and Clausewitz waited for their passports to be returned, they received an invitation from the writer and socialite, Mme de Stael, to stay at the Chateau Coppet in neutral Switzerland, by Lake Geneva. As an arch dissident she too had been exiled by Napoleon. At Coppet August's passion exploded and he met Juliette Recamier, one of the great French beauties of her time. August and Juliette fell in love and exchanged marriage vows. Napoleon too had designs on Juliette, but she had already rebuffed him. So the Prince was now Napoleon's rival in love as well as war, a cocktail with potentially fatal consequences.

Later, when reading some of the letters between August and Juliette, I found out that Juliette had changed her mind. I could see that the power of his love for Juliette was leaving August devastated. It was a shock to suddenly see the human side of the great warrior prince, to see that he was as vulnerable to the pangs of unrequited love as anyone else. Time and again he made appointments with Juliette, which she then never kept. From her responses to his letters it seemed she had ended it and would not return his great passion, but I could see from his writings just how deeply August could fall in love. It would be a pattern of behaviour that he could never forsake and I remembered Uncle Freddy telling me that the Prince had been devoted to Emilie for the last eleven years of his life.

On his return to Berlin in 1808 August was promoted to Brigadier-General and Inspector General of the whole Prussian Artillery. In contravention of the Treaty, however, he devised a plan with his generals to rebuild his army by recruiting and training 40,000 men and then sending them home before secretly recruiting another 40,000 to repeat the exercise. The Treaty forbade Prussia's army from exceeding 40,000 men. Month by month they were training a large proportion of the male population of the Empire in readiness for a return to war. August had studied the French army carefully, analysing the secrets of their success, and was applying the same rules to his own army. Without the French realising what was happening, a formidable modern army was building up under their noses. In 1812, Napoleon made his ill-judged attempt to invade Russia. Forced back by the bitter winter and the Russian army, many of his own troops drowned in the ice flows as they tried to retreat.

August described Napoleon as "that little Corsican" and it was obvious that burning inside both of them was a personal hatred for each other. As Chief of the entire Prussian Artillery, August confronted the retreating Napoleon in 1813 on the outskirts of Leipzig. Single-handedly leading his army he routed the French, creating the turning point of the whole war. I felt a great sense of pride as I read that August was one of the first Prussians to be awarded the Iron Cross for his bravery and heroism. The victorious leaders, the Russian Tsar, the Emperor of Austria and the Prussian King, rewarded August by giving him the largest captured French cannon, known as "Le Drole". It was a personal prize and a token of their gratitude and admiration.

A jubilant August transported the cannon back with him to Berlin, where it had pride of place in front of his Bellevue Palace, and remained there for 132 years. Ken and I were to discover later, when we were guests of the German government and during a private tour of the Bellevue Palace, that at the end of the Second World War General de Gaulle arrived in person in a truck. He removed the cannon and took it back to Paris where it has remained ever since.

His defeat at Waterloo was not the end for Napoleon. He was still refusing to give in, merely retreating back behind his own borders to regroup yet again. The Prussian King then appointed August as his Commander in France, ordering him to invade and capture Napoleon. In bloody hand-to-hand battles, August seized all the French fortress towns one by one and the French army, devastated by his relentless onslaught, finally called for a truce.

All through the day Herr Waltmann kept returning to see how we were getting on, and each time he came he would proudly bring another pile of papers for us. I now felt I had truly got to know the man who was destined to meet and fall in love with Emilie. My father would have been amazed to know that his daughter, the young girl whom he had trusted with the verbal family inheritance, was now opening up the dungeons of history. But would I ever be allowed to find Emilie herself? By the end of the day we felt like August had introduced us to every member of his illustrious family, but still there was no mention of Emilie or of anyone with the family name of Gottschalk. I had read about the Prince's first two morganatic marriages, to his first wife Friederike, whom he divorced, and his second wife, Auguste, but nothing after that. We found a note of Auguste dying in 1833, which would have left the Prince a widower soon after meeting Emilie, and we could find a reference to Eduard, the son of his first wife. So there would have been ten years after his second wife died of cancer in Italy when he could have been married to Emilie before he himself died in 1843, which pretty much fitted the story that had been passed down by word of mouth through our family. But if that was so and the family story was all true, why weren't Emilie and their daughter Charlotte recorded anywhere?

When Ken and I finally looked up from our studies it dawned on us that we were the only ones left in the reading room. It seemed we had become so absorbed in the stories of Prince August we hadn't even noticed everyone else leaving and going home. Reluctantly we tore ourselves away from the Hohenzollern family and made our way back to the dreary surroundings of the hotel. Although the day had been fascinating, by the time we got back to the hotel we realised that we were no closer to finding Emilie, but there was always tomorrow.

Victor, our friendly young waiter at the hotel, was eager to chat when we got down for breakfast the next morning. "I really want to travel," he whispered as he served us, his eyes darting around the room nervously. "We only get to go to the Black Sea a few weeks each year for our holidays, but I want to get to the West."

"Listen, Victor," I said, wanting to encourage him in his enthusiasm but anxious to change the subject before he started asking us to smuggle him out of the country or something else that would get us into trouble with the authorities just when we had somehow managed to get into their good books. "I love this salami sausage. Is there any chance you could find me one to take back to England with me?"

"Oh yes, of course," he grinned, happy to be able to do something to please us. "I will have it for you tomorrow."

"Victor!" the manager's voice cut across the hushed atmosphere of the room and he scurried away, looking guilty. He didn't speak to us, or even look at us, again as we ate our breakfast and talked about everything we had discovered the day before. Ken was now as obsessed with finding out what had happened to August, Emilie and Charlotte as I was and we kept going over all the possible scenarios, none of which quite seemed to fit the few facts we had gathered so far.

As soon as we had finished our breakfast we left Victor clearing the table with his eyes still discreetly averted and drove to the archive. Herr Waltmann was waiting, happily holding another mountain of files for us. By now he seemed more anxious than ever for us to find what we were looking for as we were, and just as excited by the chase. After just two days the three of us had already established our routine of working and Ken and I settled down quickly to our reading. After a few moments I picked up a scrap of paper that didn't look like anything special. I stared at it for a moment, trying to work out what it was. Then I saw the name and my heart jumped.

CHAPTER
TWELVE

Gottschalk

"Gottschalk!" I exclaimed, making Ken jump and the other readers look up disapprovingly. "I've found the name. This is a bill from August's tailor and his name is Gottschalk. Surely this must be the link. There's even an original piece of red velvet attached as a sample of a coat he had made for Friederike, August's first wife. My father had said that Emilie's father was a tailor."

I stroked the soft velvet which had been lying in amongst these papers for a century and a half but still looked as good as new, and tried to imagine the dress that it would have been made into. Emilie was wearing a beautiful red dress in the portrait that Uncle Freddy had showed me, although it wasn't possible to tell what material it was made from. Had Gottschalk the tailor made that one too? I wondered. If the dress was for August's first wife, that would have meant that the Prince knew Gottschalk when Emilie was no more than a child, maybe before she was even born. That thought raised more questions than answers.

"So, August had a Jewish tailor," Ken said, taking the fragile piece of paper from me and squinting at it closely.

"Now we've found the Gottschalks," I said, "but where is Emilie?"

"At least we know that her father was probably August's tailor," Ken replied. "Or she must have been related to him in some way. She could have been a niece or a sister, I suppose. Just knowing who the family are is a big step forward. It's all beginning to make a little more sense."

"I so much want to find her name recorded somewhere," I sighed. "Why isn't it here? I want to see their two names together in ink, to know that their relationship existed and to know why Charlotte, their child, had told my father and Uncle Freddy that her whole life had suddenly changed when she was around five years old."

Momentarily buoyed up by our find, we went back to our labours with even more enthusiasm, immersing ourselves in every minute detail of August's life. By studying his household accounts we were able to visit his palaces at Bellevue, Prillwitz and Wilhelmstrasse 65 and see exactly how they were run. Not surprisingly he had a considerable retinue of staff around him. As well as his Master of Household, he employed three adjutants and two secretaries, two valets and a personal physician. There were two cooks, a butler and a pastry cook. There were servants who were solely in charge of the silver plate and equerries to look after other precious objects, plus the appropriate numbers of lackeys, coachmen, scullery maids, stewards, chambermaids, outriders, stable boys, kitchen boys and gardeners at each establishment — the lists of staff and possessions appeared to go on forever.

The endless reams of detailed entries bore witness to just how rich the Prince was and also to what lavish parties he threw for the European royalty and nobility of the day. I even discovered one extraordinary note telling of an argument August had had with his French chef, La Notte, concerning the number of pheasants required for a particular dinner party. La Notte was making it clear to the Prince in no uncertain terms that he couldn't possibly make the numbers required in so short a time. It seemed that for once August had met his match. It seemed he was a man who took all his pleasures very seriously, including his eating. It seemed incomprehensible that a man who had had virtually every move he ever made chronicled and archived could disappear as completely as he had from the history books. Why had all this material been hidden away for so long?

He was obviously a great patron too and we came across the name of the famous architect and designer, Karl Schinkel, when August hired him to undertake the complete redesign and extension of the Wilhelmstrasse Palace for his personal comfort. The descriptions and drawings left no doubt as to just how magnificent a palace this would have been. Wilhelmstrasse 65 was a two-storey building, nineteen window-axes wide, long enough to dominate a large site halfway along the street. A ramp with a wrought-iron railing led up to the higher central section and two lofty archways in the side wings led to the courtyards which were enclosed by smaller wings housing servants, kitchens and stables. Between the wings lay a splendid garden.

Every detail of the building and decorating work on the palace, as well as details of work done on other palaces, lay in the files that we were now ploughing through. Considering how little information had been available about this Prince when I first set out on the hunt, I now felt like I was drowning in all the events and colour of August's life. It was an intoxicating feeling as I worked frantically to read and understand everything that was being put in front of me, trying to sort out the nuggets that would add to my picture of his eventual life with my great, great grandmother from all the chaff of irrelevant detail that surrounded them. It was as if the identity of the Prince himself were beginning to seep into my soul and it felt almost like I was falling in love with him, with all his grand, extravagant gestures coupled with the way he meticulously planned every detail of his life.

August had so much power and wealth, always an explosive combination, which gave him an authority that must at times have intimidated the crown. The King was an absolute ruler but a man like August with such a revered war record would have ruffled more than a few feathers.

Records showed that the Prince was also a great lover of art and sculpture. The elaborate ballroom at Wilhelmstrasse was a testament to just how high his position in European society must have been. It is hard to imagine that there could have been a more magnificent room anywhere at the time.

Then, when I least expected it, all that I had hoped for, everything I had been imagining became possible. While I was immersed in August's hectic life through his diaries, bills and household accounts, Herr Waltmann appeared behind me unexpectedly, making me sit up with a jerk as he placed another large file on the table before me. I will never forget the feeling that swept over me as I realised what it was.

At first glance it looked very much like so many of the other files we had already ploughed through, bulky with documents. I opened it and my heart leaped.

"I can't believe my eyes," I blurted out.

"What is it?" Ken asked, startled by my shout.

"It's Emilie. It must be her. Please, please let it be her. 'The Prince August of Prussia and his years with Emilie von Ostrowska', that's what it says. But she's not called Gottschalk. She's not the tailor's daughter. She's a von Ostrowska, an aristocrat."

CHAPTER
THIRTEEN

Finding Emilie

I could feel the tension and emotion building up inside my head. There were some markings on the outside cover with a number. The names were written inside, together in the same sentence at last, just as I had been dreaming about for so long. Ken clasped my hand. He could see that I was confused and peered into the file with me, looking back over a hundred years.

"This must be your Emilie, Evi. Prince August died in 1843 and your father definitely said that she spent the last eleven years of his life with him. Here is the evidence. That's all you need."

He ran his finger over the dates — "1832–1843" — written under their names. I was beginning to feel overcome with relief, but I still couldn't understand why it said Emilie's family name was von Ostrowska and not Gottschalk. Then I had an idea.

"Was this the new name she was given by the King when she married August? After all she was Jewish. She must have changed her name to be accepted into high society."

Ken remained silent, clearly as perplexed as I was. I could hear my father's voice in my head and I felt sure he was experiencing all these emotions through my eyes. Despite the fact that he had told me not to go looking I was sure he would be happy at this discovery, that he would be proud of his daughter and of what she had achieved.

"Now I've found her," I said. "I've really found my Emilie. I am so excited, Ken."

For those few moments I wanted to forget the confusion about the different names and relish the discovery for a little while longer. I wanted to shout my joy from the rooftops. It was all true, she did exist and was this file now going to tell me the whole story? I sincerely hoped so. When I turned the next page I would finally be meeting my great, great grandmother. Indulging in the moment, I pulled the pocket-book out from my bag and opened it on the page where August had inscribed the words, "the beautiful owner of this book is dearer to me than my life, August your protector."

The Prince's handwriting had grown so familiar over the previous few days of trawling through the files, and now I was finally going to find out all the things I had wanted to know for so long, the mysteries were going to be unravelled. Part of me was frightened to turn the page for fear that I would find the crucial documents had been removed or censored, but after a few seconds I opened the file while Ken watched over my shoulder. I could hear my heart thumping.

"Frau von Ostrowska . . ." August wrote on two different files.

"Ken," I said, grabbing his arm in excitement, "Ken, this is the proof he married Emilie, look at these."

I was trying to imagine the scene as I read, transporting myself back in time. I knew how anti-Semitic the Prussian Empire was so I could picture exactly how degrading the King would have found it for one of his close relatives to be consorting with a girl who was not only a commoner and the daughter of a tailor, but a Jew as well. Yet it looked as if Emilie had been awarded a title to disguise her humble origins. What would August have had to do to persuade the King to make such a concession?

We knew from the papers which covered court politics that the King would definitely have taken advice from Furst Wittgenstein, his right-hand man and a great influence on all the decisions taken at court. Wittgenstein was famous for his anti-Semitic views, as I would find out later, and would almost certainly have been against the idea of any union. Was the King rewarding August for his valiant services in defeating Napoleon? I recalled my mother telling me that morning in 1940 in our kitchen that August went ahead and married Emilie without the King's permission. Was it just that August was such an unconquerable man, and such a dominant character, that not even his monarch had a hold over him?

We had already discovered that August was an outspoken supporter of the Jews even before he met Emilie Gottschalk. His earlier papers had told us the story of a Jewish soldier called Meno Burg who had been refused entry into all the other Prussian regiments because of his religion. Those who rejected him claimed it was because he refused to swear allegiance on a bible, but in reality it was simple anti-Semitism. This had been a real revelation and an insight that reflected well on August's character and sense of justice. It seemed he was a beacon for the Jews, standing up to anti-Semitism at a time when Jews were not welcomed into the army. August was determined to have this man in the Artillery, knowing what a good officer he was, so he got him to swear his allegiance over the barrel of a gun, using the Old Testament and with a rabbi present. In the evidence I discovered he revealed how much he hated prejudice and he later asked the King to allow Burg to be promoted to become one of Prussia's first Jewish majors. August eventually went on to promote Burg to the position of Head of the Military Academy in Berlin.

Even the King, in line with the generally anti-Semitic feelings that were prevalent in Prussia at the time, was against it, but August was in such an invincible position because of his victories that the King was forced to give in to the request.

"It looks like August was already building up enemies at court by then," Ken said when he read the story. "Maybe this is why the King ordered that all these papers be locked away after August's death and insisted that his name should be erased from the history books. Furst Wittgenstein was the King's most trusted adviser at the time and he would never have favoured a Jew in that anti-Semitic climate. He would have hated Burg and would have disapproved of August's championing such a man."

It would have been an even greater risk for a member of the royal family as senior as the Prince was, to start an open relationship with a Jewish girl, but it was typical of everything we had found out about him so far that he would see no reason why he shouldn't please himself in such a choice.

"August was not a man who would have had to plead with the King for this kind of favour," Ken said. "But he would also have been in a strong position because of his popularity with his soldiers and his successes on the battlefield. But then again he had so much trouble persuading them to allow him to promote Meno Burg, it seems incredible that he managed to persuade them to ennoble a humble Jewish tailor's daughter."

We were going round and round in circles with our speculations. I opened the file and began to read. For a few moments I couldn't understand what I was being told. It was a completely different story to the one we had constructed in our heads since finding out that August's tailor was called Gottschalk.

Everything about Emilie was still shrouded in mystery. Ostrowska wasn't an awarded title as we had assumed, it was her family name. How was that possible? I read on and on, hungry for answers. Emilie's father, it seemed, wasn't a Jewish tailor at all, nor was he called Gottschalk. Emilie's real father, the records told us, was Major Adam von Ostrowski (male members of the family ended the name with an "i" while the females changed it to "a"), a well-connected

Polish aristocrat. He was a senior army figure who had formerly been in the Prince von Orien Regiment and was one of the King's trusted majors. His son Hermann, Emilie's brother, was also a high-ranking officer in the King's army.

Having been told Emilie was from a humble Jewish family we had gone on to make a string of assumptions which we could now see were entirely wrong. This was a family of considerable influence and consequence, so why had Emilie ended up becoming the Hohenzollern secret? Why had she been erased from history like this, leaving barely a trace? All our theories about it being due to anti-Semitism appeared to have been a long way wide of the mark; something else must have happened to cause her relegation to historical oblivion.

Emilie von Ostrowska's mother, we would later discover, had passed away when Emilie was still a small child, so she would probably have been closer to her father than most girls of that age and class, and might well have been known personally to the King. Not only was her father a Major of Polish descent, but we had also discovered that her brother, Hermann, was a highly decorated officer in the King's army. If we had not found this out, we might have convinced ourselves that Emilie had taken on a new name to hide her Jewish origins. However now we knew that she was not a humble tailor's daughter but the child of a highly distinguished family, so how had it come about that Emilie's true origins had been so carefully hidden? And how had August and Emilie's daughter, Charlotte, come to bear the name of Gottschalk when none of them had anything to do with the Gottschalk family? There was of course the connection between August and Isadore Gottschalk, since we knew that Isadore was the Prince's tailor. We had the evidence for that in the form of that lush piece of rich velvet and the bill Isadore had rendered. I knew that both Uncle Freddy and my father had been certain that Emilie's father was a Jewish tailor, because they had told me so. This new information, however, suggested they were wrong and that had made the puzzle even greater. I realised that I was nowhere nearer solving it than I had been the day I arrived in Merseburg.

"So, Emilie wasn't Jewish at all," Ken said as I relayed the story to him in whispers. "That means Charlotte wasn't either."

Both of us were thinking the same thing. This meant that Charlotte's daughter, my grandmother Anna who had almost certainly died at the hands of the Nazis, couldn't have been Jewish either.

"No," I said, as I was trying to piece it all together in my head at the same time as he was. "And yet the Nazis caused Anna's death," Ken said. "And if they did, then they killed a direct descendant of the Prussian royal family, a historical family that Hitler had the greatest respect for. He actually claimed that he modelled himself on Frederick the Great. The King's picture was hanging in Hitler's bunker when he finally committed suicide. So why would the Nazi high command have allowed that to happen to Anna? How could such a tragedy have come about? Why would she not have told them who she was in order to save herself?"

134

"Because the Nazis believed she was a Gottschalk and so did she," I said, thinking out loud. "Just as we did. They thought she was Jewish and she didn't believe she had the evidence to prove otherwise. Just like my father. Anna may have always believed the story about her grandmother being a Gottschalk before she married the Prince."

I noticed my hands were shaking slightly, making the ancient sheets of paper rattle a little in my fingers. Why had my father and all those who had come before him insisted that Emilie was known as a Gottschalk? And where was Emilie's daughter Charlotte going to fit into this story? She was now the missing link between Emilie and Anna, the daughter of one and mother of the other. What had happened to create the terrible situation that probably ended my grandmother's life so tragically and unnecessarily?

CHAPTER
FOURTEEN

Going to the Ball

We were again going round and round in circles with our questions and as we were only too aware how little time we had in the Merseburg Archive, we put aside our speculations for the moment and went back to reading. I was excited to have discovered that Emilie von Ostrowska was in fact my great, great grandmother and I was now being whisked back more than a century to the actual scene where the incredible love story between Emilie and August started.

Berlin must have been full of stories about the balls that August threw, with much gossiping about the daughters of officers and the pretty girls from the city of Berlin who he invited. He was the first to introduce the waltz to Berlin and would invite members of the public in to watch the dancing. La Notte, his famous chef, was reported to lay on sumptuous buffets for the guests.

I imagined myself being there. It was 1832 and I was in the Prince's grand ballroom, at one of his most lavish balls. I had now actually arrived at the place and time where they met, there at the heart of Berlin's social scene, in the fabulous Wilhelmstrasse Palace designed by the famous architect and painter, Karl Schinkel. I was meeting the young Fraulein Ostrowska for the first time.

It may well have been the first high society event that Emilie had ever attended and we knew from having read so much about August's domestic arrangements, that it would have been a dazzling affair. The grand staircase would have been lavishly decorated with flowers and white silk blinds would have been lowered in front of the mighty windows. There would have been three sparkling crystal chandeliers hanging from the ceiling, their light multiplied by the mirrors on the walls in between the lapis lazuli pillars. The side walls of the room were lined with crimson sofa seats and two open mahogany doors would have displayed the great dining room where fleets of servants put their finishing touches to the small round tables where the guests would later be taking supper, the violet tones of the walls set off by the white of the tables and chairs. More tables and sideboards had been set up in adjoining rooms to ensure that everyone could be seated, all laid out with silver from the royal plate room as well as with a hundred of August's own silver plates; the Blue Room, its walls covered in luminous silk interwoven with small yellow stars, its sofas and chairs upholstered in white silk, and the State Room with its crimson damask walls and heavy white curtains.

I visualised the crowds of partygoers as they strolled from room to room, drinking in the intricate decorative details. One room was dominated by a life-sized portrait of a woman we had already read about, the famous beauty, Juliette Recamier, one of the few women who had been able to hold the Prince's affections for many years, despite rejecting him as a lover. Most of the sophisticated crowd would have heard the rumours and smiled discreetly to one another when they saw the portrait.

It would have been hard for any young girl to resist being swept off her feet by the attentions of such a famous man in such glamorous surroundings. Prince August was not only one of the wealthiest men ever to have lived in Europe, he was also a war hero and a larger than life character. It would be the equivalent these days of one of Hollywood's most famous and established stars setting his sights on a star-struck young actress attending her first adult party.

I could imagine all too clearly how worried Major Ostrowski must have been when watching his beautiful daughter happily dancing the night away with a handsome prince, a powerful and celebrated man in his early fifties who had already been married twice. By all accounts August's interest in Emilie was matched by her interest in him, so her father would have been able to see that August was clearly sweeping the young girl off her feet. In Major Ostrowski's eyes Emilie would still have been little more than a child and yet he would suddenly have been forced to see her as a woman who could turn the head of a dangerous and exciting man, a man who could pretty much demand whatever he wanted. Was the Major wishing he hadn't allowed Emilie to attend the ball that night? If I had been him I couldn't say now, with my hand on my heart, that that thought wouldn't have been foremost in my mind.

I could also imagine the King's great displeasure with the idea of his Major's daughter being seduced by a man whose personal lifestyle he did not approve of, however much he might admire his skills as a soldier and leader.

Perhaps if she had had a mother to go to for advice, Emilie would have been persuaded to be more circumspect about giving away her love, and her life, to a man with August's long and colourful history. It is unlikely however, that her father, a military man, could easily have known how to find the words to advise a fifteen-year-old daughter on such delicate and private matters involving a Hohenzollern Prince.

As we found out more, Ken and I soon realised that Emilie had lost her heart almost the first moment that the Prince asked her to dance that night in Berlin by the light of thousands of flickering candles. It was also obvious that for different reasons August was just as smitten with Emilie as she was with him. He was a lover of all the good things in life, including beautiful women, which was another reason why he was not liked by the more conservative members of the Royal Court, like Wittgenstein. It seemed that the moment he set eyes on Emilie, August was unable to stop himself from pursuing her, even though he must have known from the beginning that a liaison with a man like himself was likely to be fraught with complications for a young girl.

I dare say he was a man who was used to getting exactly what he wanted whenever he wanted it, and there didn't seem to be much time between that first meeting and the moment when August and Emilie had set the whole of Berlin talking about their relationship. News travelled fast in those days and gossip was always rife, especially about the royal family. After lengthy negotiations with Major Ostrowski, Prince August announced to the world that he was going to marry Emilie.

The records contained an account by Prince Wilhelm, the son of King Frederick Wilhelm III, which told us that on the day the betrothal was announced she emerged from her home in a beautiful white dress with a garland of lilies in her hair, looking every inch a princess. She was carried to August in the golden coach he had sent to collect her. A small crowd of on-lookers had gathered outside his house in Jaegerstrasse, a normally private and secluded residence, to witness her arrival. It must have seemed that Emilie was going to live a life straight out of any number of children's fairy stories or cautionary tales. I still couldn't understand why such a romantic and dramatic story had been buried so deeply in the vaults at Merseburg, and only ever been whispered about in our own family. Surely it must have been widely talked and written about by commentators at the time? The one last thing I had to do that night was to tell the boys that we had found Emilie. Phoning from the East was very difficult, so I proudly put the news down on a postcard. I knew just how excited they would be.

I thought about my granny Anna, as I often did. Her terrible fate, it seemed, had been sealed that wedding day more than one hundred years earlier in nineteenth-century Prussia. As she died at the hands of the Nazis, did she know the true identity of her grandmother? She couldn't have, I thought, since my father and Uncle Freddy didn't seem to know. I shuddered at the very thought, because it had become quite clear to me that there was no way Anna could have saved herself when they finally came for her.

Seeing that I was upset by the pictures in my imagination, Ken gently took my arm and signalled that it was time for us to leave for the night.

CHAPTER
FIFTEEN

An Assassin in the Palace and the Disappearance of Victor

Prince August was an intelligent man and the more I read about him the more I realised that there were many sides to his character. A man of principle, he had proved his friendship to the Jews by arguing with the King in his defence of his officer, Meno Burg. He was also a maverick reformer, Prussia's "new broom" in many ways. Unlike any other member of the Royal family, August entertained new ideas and held great hope for the future. I could see why Emilie would have been attracted to a man with such buccaneering qualities, someone who was quite prepared to thumb his nose at authority and go against convention when he believed it was the right thing to do.

It was hardly surprising that a man like August had enemies, maybe even deliberately creating them if he felt strongly about something, after all he lived in a society where power and control meant everything. Through her innocence and the deep love that had ensnared her, Emilie had stumbled into a situation that she could never have been able to predict. The Prince, however, would have known only too well what dangers lay ahead and from the moment when they vowed to spend the rest of their lives together, he seemed to become almost paranoid about his young wife's safety.

"I can understand it to a point, Ken," I said, thinking aloud. "Emilie is the love of his life and therefore very precious to him, and if he was this great visionary who was never afraid to stand up and be counted, there could well have been enemies who would have harboured thoughts of getting to him by harming her."

Emilie's sister, Helena, accompanied her whenever August went away to fulfil his duties as Artillery Inspector to the Prussian army. Reading his journals, I realised that he was travelling almost constantly around the Empire. Even when he was with her, however, August would be watching over her safety constantly, sending his aides out to check the gardens before even allowing Emilie to go outside for a walk. All visitors, if uninvited, were summarily turned away from the house without being allowed to see her, particularly whenever she was staying in his Palace in Prillwitz.

Who, I wondered, would have been the main suspects behind these threats to August and Emilie? My suspicions pointed me to the monarch himself, King Frederick William III.

"Emilie was obviously a problem for the King," I told Ken, thinking out loud over supper as I often did. "We can see from the records that she was never mentioned at any of the events that Prince August was reported to have attended. My mother told me that the marriage was morganatic after my father first showed me the pocket-book, so could there have been a connection to that? I think I know why she lived in the grand apartment August had acquired for them as a private residence in Jaegerstrasse. Why was she treated differently to his first two wives? It all suggests that August must have married Emilie without the King's permission, that the union was taboo. But why on earth would that be?"

I had been wrestling with the discovery that Emilie was Major Adam von Ostrowski's daughter and trying to get used to the fact that the family folklore was wrong. I had now accepted that my great-great grandmother was Emilie von Ostrowska and that she was not Jewish. And even if theirs was a forbidden love, as it seemed to be, it was obvious that my golden couple were not prepared to give each other up, no matter how much their enemies tried to intimidate them. But while August was not afraid to stand up to any amount of danger when it came to his own safety, it seemed he was acutely aware of just how vulnerable his young wife was in the long months when he was away from her.

August's closest and most trusted aide was his secretary, Uhde, who was also his Privy Councillor. The Prince insisted that Uhde be at Emilie's side at all times when he wasn't able to be there himself, especially when she travelled to the Prillwitz Palace, where he seemed to believe the threats to her life were the most pressing. The Palace was about a hundred kilometres from Berlin in the middle of nowhere and very isolated. It was an area where a lot of hunting went on.

The archives gave a startling insight into just how concerned the Prince was as he oversaw every move his young wife made. August was Emilie's protector; he was acting out the promise that he made to her when he wrote those words in the pocket-book that had been passed down the generations to me.

When the doctor suggested that Emilie needed to travel to a spa for her health, the Prince suggested she should go to Interlaken, which would involve crossing several frontiers. He could not accompany her himself and so ordered Uhde to travel with her and with her sister and their servants. Worried about the safety of such a vulnerable young girl, he drew up a list of instructions for the journey so detailed that it stretched to an extraordinary twenty pages. As I read through them I felt moved by the fact that he was so loving and cared so much about her, but at the same time I could imagine how overwhelmed and confined she must have felt at times by the intense love of this man who wanted to protect every minute detail of her life, even from a distance.

"Someone should be at the side of a young lady like Frau von Ostrowska, to whom His Royal Highness is very tenderly attached," the document announced. "Someone who pays attention to all that is required for her physical and moral well-being, someone who will make sure that, with regard to the high costs of such a journey, money is spent economically."

The Prince then launched into details about exactly what should happen regarding Emilie's medical care should she fall ill on the journey, and financial details of the money to be taken and how the accounts should be kept.

"In order to safeguard the passports and money for the journey whilst the party is staying in inns," the Prince continued, "they should be carried in a strongbox which is to be fixed to the floor in the different rooms they occupy by means of a screw inside the box."

The coach, harnessed up with four post horses, which were to be changed at every staging post, was to leave as early as possible each morning, but never whilst it was still dark, and on no account was the postillion to leave it unattended. The post horses were to be paid for in Prussian currency and the coach was to be greased at least three times per day and was to drive more slowly whenever the roads were stony. Emilie was to decide how long they should travel each day and a comfortable break was to be arranged during the midday heat. Bad roads and areas in which "cholera, brigands, floods or other hazardous circumstances" might be expected were to be avoided as far as possible. Uhde was to examine inns and private quarters to make sure they were clean and orderly before Emilie entered them. Finally, the Prince gave the official travel companion a special duty:

If anything that might be damaging to Frau von Ostrowska's reputation or that might possibly offend against outward propriety should at any time occur or seem about to occur, Uhde should raise the strongest objections and do his utmost to see to it that his counsel be followed in order to deflect the threat, whether past or present.

Besides all this Uhde also had to make sure that Emilie neither paid nor received any visits and did not participate in public events at the spas, except where it was unavoidable. She was only to "visit such public places in which a young lady may respectably appear" and where possible she was to avoid making acquaintances, especially among "younger people".

It seems likely that the Prince, being aware of just how wide the age gap was between them, felt jealous of the thought of Emilie in the company of men younger and perhaps more handsome than himself. He suggested that should she feel the need for company then Uhde should be the one to provide it. Uhde was also charged with the task of writing weekly reports in the course of the journey. If he could not find the time then he should ask Emilie to do this for him. Apparently there was no doubt in the Prince's mind that their union would put Emilie's life in danger.

As Emilie wasn't, as we had originally assumed, Jewish and was in fact from a noble Polish family, it was hard to see why anyone apart from her own family and the King would object that vehemently to the relationship, let alone strongly enough to want to attack or kill her. Unless of course it was because their marriage posed some sort of threat to the Crown and to the succession. Was it possible that that was why August might assume that the royal establishment would be keen to get rid of her?

Every time we found an answer to one question, two new ones seemed to spring up in its place. There was no option but to keep reading and hope that we would come up with more clues as we ploughed on through the endless documents. A few hours later I received my next shock.

"Oh my God," I exclaimed out loud, trying to read on and talk at the same time in my excitement. "They tried to poison Emilie. It's all here. Someone slipped methylated spirits into her wine glass while August was away and she was holidaying at the Prillwitz Palace."

August had always thought that Prillwitz carried more dangers to his young bride than the other palaces and his fears had been proved right. It was a terrifying moment and I became desperately concerned as I read that the staff called out August's personal doctor, a Dr Barez, to tend to her, while the Prince himself rushed back from wherever he had been inspecting the troops to be with her the moment he heard the news. I was turning the pages with frantic speed, desperate to find out if she would survive, fearing that I was about to lose her, and when she was still so young. I could imagine how agonising that trip home must have been for August, he would have been beside himself, his worst fears having come true. Not knowing if she would be dead before he got there or whether he would be there in time to tell her how much he loved her before she faded, every hour must have felt like an age.

I was so relieved I almost cheered out loud when I found reports that she had survived the attempt on her life and was already regaining her strength by the time her husband's carriage rattled through the gates of Prillwitz. By that stage she and August had been together for six years, which appeared to prove that their relationship was about more than mere mutual infatuation. Perhaps that was why the attempt had been made on her life. Was it possible that at the beginning their enemies had assumed the relationship wouldn't last and when they realised their mistake they decided they had to take other measures to end it? But still I couldn't understand why anyone would feel so strongly about a marriage between a distinguished man and a young girl from a good family, that they would want to murder her. Was it possible that this was the time she fell pregnant with Charlotte? The dates could easily fit. Thinking about Charlotte made me wonder why they hadn't had any children already. Ken was quite dogmatic when I wondered out loud.

"I am not surprised that they held off from having any children," he said. "It's obvious that they had enough on their plate as it was. And if they were to bring a child into the world, what kind of danger would it find itself in? It seems unlikely that they would want to do that."

But bring a child into the world they did, because it couldn't have been long after the attempt on Emilie's life that my great grandmother, Charlotte, was born, in what must have been very dangerous circumstances. Was the birth planned? We knew that August was a fearless operator who courted, even welcomed danger, if only so he could prove how infallible he was, with a resolve so hard that he would beat off any attempt to damage him. He had proved that when facing Napoleon; that was the ultimate test. Things were different this time though because it wasn't just his life that was at stake, but the lives of his wife and new baby.

"August must have prevented Emilie from becoming pregnant until then, Ken," I observed. "Six years is a long time, their love was deep, and the urge to produce a child between them must have been very powerful."

However much August might have wanted to stay with Emilie and protect her after such a frightening ordeal, his duties, both as a royal prince and a soldier, made it impossible and it wasn't long before another attempt was made on Emilie's life. The opportunity came while the Prince was away again on a ship near Turkey. It happened when Emilie and Uhde were travelling back to Berlin from Prillwitz and Emilie's coach came under attack. There was a graphic account in the archive of the horses rearing up noisily as the driver desperately whipped them forward in order to make his escape from the attackers and the police were involved. My heart was in my mouth as I followed the account. I felt like I was living through the terrifying ordeal myself, hardly able to breathe until I saw confirmation that she had somehow managed to survive.

★ ★ ★

By the end of yet another day of burrowing in the archives we had discovered more about my family than I had ever dreamed possible when I first set out on the search, which left me feeling elated. But at the same time we had a hundred new questions in our heads as well and I wanted to keep working until I had answered every one of them. If the archive hadn't been closing for the night I don't know if Ken would have been able to tear me away from that desk until I eventually fell asleep over the files. As it was I had no choice but to leave with everyone else, my mind still buzzing from everything I was learning.

When Ken and I got back to the hotel we found a different waiter at our table in the dining room.

"Where's Victor?" I asked the new man. "Isn't he working this evening?"

"Victor no longer works here," he said, avoiding my eyes, obviously not wanting to elaborate any more than that.

"They're watching us," Ken said quietly as the waiter walked away from the table.

I was too taken up with all my own thoughts about the day's findings to give his suggestion any serious consideration. Knowing how nervous he was about being behind the Iron Curtain, I thought he was probably imagining it. All through the meal I chattered excitedly on about August and Emilie and all the possible scenarios that might have led to what eventually befell poor Anna. If he was still thinking about the missing Victor, Ken did a good job of hiding it and of being just as fascinated as I was by my family's past trials and tribulations. After dinner we went up to our room, exhausted from our long day's work and found that someone had hung a small chimney sweep doll on the wall.

"Oh look, Ken," I said innocently. "How sweet. I hear they're meant to bring good luck."

"Are they now?" Ken said noncommittally as he went over and peered at the ornament without touching it. Turning back to me he put his finger to his lips and I watched as he picked up a piece of paper and wrote a single word on it. "Bug".

"You think so?" I said, wondering if perhaps he was being a little paranoid when everything seemed to be going so well and everyone was being so helpful.

Ken then blurted out loudly, in a puzzling change of subject. "It's not like home, is it? I haven't seen a single piece of fruit the whole time I've been here."

He put his finger to his lips again to stop me asking what on earth he was talking about and we went to bed without saying anything else that was likely to cause us any problems. Although his suspicions were making me uncomfortable it wasn't long before my mind had drifted back to the mysteries of Emilie and her disappearing daughter, Charlotte. That night there had been nothing for us to do apart from mull over whatever we had discovered that day, trying out possible different explanations on one another, trying to imagine what it must have been like to be in August and Emilie's position.

Despite his inability to resist every pretty face that came along, there was no doubt of the strength of the bond of love that existed between them. Emilie was obviously willing to put her life in the most immediate danger in order to remain with August. She could easily have left him at any stage, but never did. Had she come from a poorer background, had she been the daughter of an impoverished tailor as we had first assumed, then we might have suspected she was willing to put up with the danger in order to win the security and privileges of great wealth. But now we knew she came from a secure and wealthy background it seemed unlikely that whatever August could offer her would have been enough to make the risks and sacrifices worthwhile. Had she married a nobleman of her own rank she would have been able to live a completely open and carefree life, able to move freely about in society with all the money she could have wanted but without any of the worries of assassination or of making enemies at Court. The only possible explanation for them having been together for so many years was that she was as deeply in love with him as he was with her.

But where were the birth and existence of Charlotte recorded? How were we going to find out what happened to my great grandmother that changed her life so radically when she was five years old, as she had told my father and uncle? My thoughts were still spinning round and round in circles when I eventually succumbed to sleep.

The following morning when we went down to breakfast Ken grinned triumphantly as we walked into the dining room and saw small bowls of fruit sitting on some of the tables. Coincidence or not, the experience was unnerving.

"You see?" he hissed smugly. "They were listening. We can't be complacent, Eve, or forget for one moment where we are."

There was nothing I could say. He had proved his point. I could tell that he was growing increasingly nervous about being in a totalitarian country and was anxious to get me back to the safety of the West as quickly as possible. I, on the other hand, was now so hooked on the story of Emilie and August that I wanted to stay until I had drained every last piece of information from the files. But the events at our hotel were concerning me. Although I played it down with Ken, the bug in our room made me realise that it was time for us to leave. This was indeed a dangerous place and it wouldn't be right or fair to ask him to extend our stay.

The following morning Ken and I were back at our table in the reading room as soon as the archives opened their doors, not wanting to miss a single moment of the little time we had left. I was beginning to find the name of August's doctor cropping up more often in the papers I was studying. However it was no longer Emilie who was causing the doctor concern. Dr Barez wrote that he was worried about the Prince's "wheezing". The Prince was a man in his sixties by then, who had led a full and active life. It was likely that he made great demands of his body and few concessions to the passing years.

I wondered what remedies they had in the middle of the nineteenth century for breathing problems; probably not that many. The Doctor wanted him to rest and to give up some of his travel commitments, but reported that August was having none of it, and becoming impatient with the very idea of not fulfilling all his duties as normal. If that was what was going to be the death of him, he told the Doctor, then so be it. It was easy to imagine the bluff impatience a man like that would have had with anything he thought smacked of softness or defeatism. August had convinced me that he would fight on until the day he dropped. He was a lover and liver of life, and it also occurred to me that the man that I had got to know so well over the previous few days had almost certainly convinced himself that he was invincible. He could probably never envisage that dying was an option. Perhaps that was how he managed to survive Napoleon's relentless pursuit of victory on the battlefield. Against all the odds he had survived everything that the French had thrown at him. Maybe as he brushed aside all the advice he was being given by Dr Barez, he simply imagined himself as the young and virile 27-year-old officer that he once was, carrying out his duties for his beloved Prussia.

It was at this point that I came upon a document that took me completely by surprise and filled me with both sadness and a deep foreboding. On the morning of 19 July 1843, Prince August died.

CHAPTER
SIXTEEN

The Death of the Prince

It is always a shock to hear that someone has passed away, even when you're already aware that they are sick, but I had to admit to Ken I took it very badly. I was as shaken to read about this event from more than 130 years earlier as I would have been to hear that a close living relative had suddenly left us. Although it was history that I was reading I felt much more than a mere stab of grief for my great, great grandfather and a terrible sympathy for the vulnerable young widow he was leaving behind. August had invaded my life. My relationship with him had developed at an alarming rate, having started like a blind date the day I entered the archive at Merseburg.

When I found the official papers describing what had happened they told me that the Prince had been preparing to inspect his troops after raising himself from a troubled night's sleep and his heart simply gave out under the strain. Dr Barez carried out an autopsy in order to establish the cause of death and found that all the Prince's organs were sound. His body was still unusually strong and muscular and his brown hair showed hardly a streak of white in it. But in his lungs and respiratory passages there were accumulations of phlegm, which must have signified pneumonia, which had finally interfered with his breathing. I felt like I had been personally bereaved and that August had been cheated of his old age in the same way my father had.

"What about poor Emilie?" I whispered to Ken. "Where is she? How will she cope without him there to protect her? How do you suppose she got to hear about his death?"

Diving back into the files we found the answer; Emilie had been waiting in the spa town of Marienbad for August to join her for a break. It must have seemed like a safe place for her to be because Uhde was not with her. So it was he who arrived in the carriage that she had expected would be bringing August to spend a few happy days with her. Emilie guessed something serious must have happened the moment she saw Uhde stepping off the coach alone, his face grave at the prospect of breaking the tragic news to her. It must have been the most terrible shock for her.

A harrowing, vacant feeling came over me; I couldn't quite grasp what had happened. My heart ached for Emilie. She hadn't been with August when he died, and in the commentary I found in the files on his funeral she was absent too.

"Ken, if Emilie was not allowed to accompany August at official functions," I said, "she must have been barred from the funeral as well."

I could imagine just how devastating that must have been for her at such a terrible time. The man for whom she had given up her whole life had gone, leaving her with their young daughter, Charlotte. I so much wanted to comfort her, to hold her as tightly as I could, and tell her how deeply I felt her loss. I imagined the inconsolable, lonely figure wrapping herself up to escape prying eyes, ostracised by the King and presumably by the whole family, silently watching the grand procession from the side of the road. I could feel her desolation; so vulnerable standing there in the rain as the coffin passed her by, carrying the man she had loved for eleven years, frightened of what would become of her and Charlotte, while the ruthless and powerful Hohenzollern family, who had never accepted her, paraded past in all their pomp and finery.

According to the official accounts in the files, the coffin's journey back to Berlin took a stately two days and the rain poured down relentlessly according to witnesses from the time, making the torches smoky and buffeting the flags of the deputations who gathered in the towns along the way, soaking the uniforms of the garrison who had come to pay their last respects. At the Stralau Gate the Commander of Berlin was awaiting the funeral procession, which then proceeded on to the Bellevue Palace with all military honours, where the coffin was placed on the catafalque. Ten days later, on a warm summer's day, the solemn internment took place in a building called the Dome. Once again the impressive procession made its way through the streets; eight horses draped in black pulling the hearse. As principal mourner, August's nephew, Prince Wilhelm Radziwill, followed the hearse in front of the princes of the royal family.

During the service in the Dome the Court Preacher, Dr Ehrenberg, gave the funeral oration and praised August's brilliant deeds in battle, his devotion to duty, his straightforwardness and his care for his family.

"His faults did not escape rebuke," Ehrenberg continued, "and seldom did rebuke try a man more harshly than the man who ever impounded for himself anything which he desired."

The thunder of the cannon and the salvos of the Infantry completely drowned the blessing of the body and the bells tolled as the mourners left the church. Meno Burg, whose destiny August had done so much to shape, said that "in him I have lost a father". The Jews of Berlin mourned the loss of their "dear friend". The coffin was then lowered into the vault next to his parents and brothers.

The King later issued a sharp rebuke to Dr Ehrenberg for daring to speak publicly in such a way about a member of the royal family, although it is certain that he and the rest of the family would have privately agreed with the preacher's words. August has indeed "impounded anything which he desired" whether it was great palaces or beautiful young women. The preacher responded that because of his personal devotion to the Prince he had meant by his words "judge not, that ye be not judged", and the matter was allowed discreetly to drop. Berliners in the street were quoted as saying that St Peter would need to bring the 11,000 virgins to a place of safety before he should risk opening the gate of heaven to the Prince. His reputation as a womaniser must have been widespread, but it seems it did nothing to diminish his popularity.

The full extent of August's wealth, stated in the papers as being between eight and ten million taler, shocked the public and it was widely written that he was the wealthiest man in Prussia.

It is hard to imagine how anyone could have been so unkind to Emilie, who seemed such a kind and caring soul. There seemed no doubt that August was the love of her life, but he was also her protector; now her protector had gone. She still had an ally in Uhde, of course, and she still had her father's protection to fall back on should she need it, but she also had some powerful enemies at the Royal Court, particularly Prince Wittgenstein, who had still never forgiven August for his promotion of Meno Burg to become one of Prussia's first Jewish majors. It seemed likely that King Frederick William IV, who had ascended the throne only three years earlier despite being well into his forties, was probably not feeling entirely secure about the position and that he saw Emilie as a threat. Perhaps August's surviving family from his first two wives had also conspired against her together with the King, a prudent, conservative man, although not as reactionary as his father. The King and the Prince had not got on well. In fact, the Prince's relationship with the whole of the King's family was never particularly close and it was only August's duty to be present on all official occasions like parades, receptions, inaugurations and reviews that kept him in constant touch with the King's court.

It became obvious as we read on that things very quickly became bad for Emilie from the moment she was widowed. Upon his death August's own royal court, consisting of his servants, friends and courtiers, was taken over by Eduard von Waldenburg, the son of his first wife. Emilie, it seemed, was out in the social wilderness.

As if all that wasn't enough for the poor young woman to have to contend with, we then discovered that her father, who was well over seventy years old and had been growing frail for some time, suddenly dropped dead of a heart attack. By now Emilie must have been shattered by events, fate having conspired so cruelly against her. The collapse of her whole world was complete when, as we found out in another document, Uhde also died a few weeks later. During her years with August she had been allowed no other friends or allies, so now there was no one left who could help or advise her on how best to negotiate with the royal family and the Prince's court. She was left completely alone with Charlotte and unprotected in a dangerous world, knowing from past experience that there were powerful people who wished her dead so profoundly that they had already shown themselves to be willing to commission people to murder her.

When I found a note describing how August loved to romp around, "playing games with his children" it reminded me of how my father and Uncle Freddy had said that their grandmother, Charlotte, had told them how much her father, "the Prince", enjoyed playing rough games with her on the floor of their Berlin apartment. Charlotte had also told them that she was really a "duchess" and only rode in "first-class carriages", and that she was "about five years old" when her whole life had changed. I did some calculations and worked out that when this disaster struck Emilie's child would have been about five years old, so the dates fitted. But although I knew she must have existed, I was still unable to find any record of Charlotte in the files, or any details of what might have happened that changed her life so radically that she was still able to remember it when she was an older woman and a grandmother. I now had so much wonderful detail about August and Emilie's lives together that I was completely bewildered by the absence of any mention of their mystery child.

August was dead now. He had left us and, although my hurt was profound, I knew I had to regain my composure and accept the truth. It wasn't going to be easy though, simply to pick up the story again and leave him behind. How could it be? August was a man who had meant the world to Emilie, and now here I was, all these years later, trying to distance myself from the emotional quagmire that was threatening to devour her. I had to concentrate and finish the job I had come to do. We couldn't remain in East Germany indefinitely, despite the generosity shown to me by the Minister. Besides, the walls of the archive felt as though they were closing in on us. As the days went by the whole atmosphere felt more and more asphyxiating. Spending hours and days on end with our heads buried in papers was an unhealthy existence as well as an intoxicating one.

Ken knew the emotions that I was going through and he also knew how to shake me out of it. "Faith moves a mountain," he said. "We have come here to do a job, Eve, and so far so good."

In our world we had always made the best of what we had. Our journeys in life had taught us that that was the only way to think and behave, a sort of survival mentality. When the going gets tough the only way to go is forward, to be positive. Whatever the reasons for the terrible situation Emilie was in, and whatever we were going to finally come away with, August had not only taught me so much about his life but also about mine. Meeting him in those archives was to have a lifelong effect on me.

I was immersed in reading about September 1843, just two months after he died, when I came across a letter that stunned me into silence.

CHAPTER
SEVENTEEN

A Humble Plea

I wasn't able to find the words to attract Ken's attention. I was internalising the moment as I imagined the grief-stricken Emilie picking up a quill pen and writing the letter that now lay in front of me. The tip of her quill must have been thick because the ink on the page still retained its dark richness after so many years. The letter was addressed personally to the King of Prussia. My fingers were actually trembling as I lifted it reverently from the file. The writing was stylish and delicate, it reminded me so much of Granny Anna's writing, the grammar perfect. Emilie was pleading with her monarch for mercy.

I humbly ask His Majesty to please allow me to be known as "Frau von Ostrowska" (Mrs) as I have been known throughout my years with Prince August of Prussia. The granting of this most humble request is of the highest importance to the whole of my future; I acknowledge my youthful guilt, and the great suffering I caused myself during my life with the Prince, because of my love, since inclination and youthful inexperience had decided on the fate of a 15-year-old motherless child. My own instinct is that I should not need to defend myself as I never strayed from the path of virtue; the sole consolation I can find now is in honouring the memory of the man for whom I have sacrificed everything because I have loved him with youthful ecstasy. I fervently hope that through the granting of this request the world will judge me with indulgence . . .

I understood as I read it that if Emilie was not allowed to keep the title of "Frau", and if she was not allowed to be known as August's widow, her fall in social status would be terrible for her to bear. Emilie's passion, her whole being, stood naked before my eyes. I knew her, I understood her. I realised how she felt, the loss and the dangers she was facing up to. I had become Emilie and I could see myself writing that same letter, waiting with bated breath to receive a response. I understood that it was love and not money that drove her heart.

I was finally able to speak to my husband across the oblong desk.

"Ken, I've found a vital document. Emilie is pleading with the King. She knows that without his agreement she and Charlotte are in real danger. It's a desperate letter. She obviously feels terrified and exposed and totally at the mercy of the King, who has absolute power in matters of this nature. If she cannot continue to be known as the wife of Prince August her change in status will have a serious effect on Emilie's life and then on Charlotte's, I'm sure of it."

Ken said nothing, simply holding out his hand for the letter and reading it in silence.

As he read I went back to the file to look for a reply from the King, with my heart in my mouth. Would the King hold out at least some sort of lifeline to her, showing her some kindness in her hour of need? There didn't seem to be anything. I dug deeper — and then I found what I was looking for.

The document seemed innocuous enough, there was not much written on it, perhaps that was why it nearly escaped my attention. It was the reply, although not from the King, which must have been what Emilie had hoped for. The short note was a devastating rebuff, a reply of enormous significance to the future of the desolate young woman who had written honestly and passionately about how she had "loved August with youthful ecstasy". The note was written and signed in Wittgenstein's own hand and was stark in its underlying warning. I could hardly believe the cruelty of its tone. Prince Wittgenstein had written just eight words in reply to her eloquent plea for mercy.

Your request remains unconsidered by his Gracious Majesty.

This dismissal of her vital request would have demolished Emilie. It would have signified the imminent collapse of her entire world. The two lines confirmed that she was no longer the respectable widow of the Prince, left with the responsibility to bring up their child alone. Instead the last vestiges of any connection she might have had with August were severed and destroyed in an instant. After eleven years of living as the wife of a royal prince she was suddenly cast completely adrift by everyone. I dived back into the papers to try to find out what happened next. What did she do? Where did she go? Who did she turn to for help? And where, oh where was Charlotte, her child?

I couldn't find anything. There was a gaping black hole in the middle of the archive. We had been searching through those files all week and now our time in East Germany was up. Emilie's letter to the King was an incredible climax, but it had left us hanging over a cliff of uncertainty. We had managed to find Emilie and get to know how she had met Prince August and some of their life together, but something of huge significance must have happened after August's death to end up with my poor grandmother disappearing during the Holocaust in Europe. We had arrived in Merseburg believing that Emilie, and consequently Charlotte, had been of Jewish descent. If anything, the things we had discovered had deepened the mystery surrounding my family rather than shedding any light onto it.

I could hardly bear the thought of walking away before I had managed to read every single document in the files. How I longed to prolong our stay.

"You've found your great, great grandmother now," Ken reminded me when I said how much I still wanted to know. "That was what you came here to do."

I weighed it up; armed with all these documents and the proof that we had discovered, perhaps there was a real chance that we could uncover more evidence from other archives in the West. It did feel that it was time to go and I nodded my agreement, suppressing any urge to stay for longer. We were due to drive back to the West that evening and the archive would be closing in a couple of hours. I had to find a way of getting access to the material for longer so that I could study it properly. All through the week of our searching I had been marking documents that I wanted to read in more depth, away from the pressures of that reading room with the feeling of being watched every moment of every day. I really wanted to take as much of the material as possible in copied form back to the West with me. I wanted to be able to produce it as proof for all the people who had helped me with my researches at the beginning, who had faced all the same frustrations that I had faced, but it also had immense personal value to me and my family. It was evidence that had taken a lifetime to uncover.

"How many documents have I marked?" I asked Herr Waltmann when he came in to enquire if there was anything more he could do for us.

"Two hundred and seventy five," he replied without a flicker of emotion crossing his face. He had obviously been keeping a running daily total. "Is there anything else we can do for you, Mrs Haas?"

"Herr Waltmann," I put on the sweetest smile I could manage, "you have been so helpful. I really do appreciate all the assistance that you have given to me. This means so much to me. We need to take copies of these marked documents away with us. Can you arrange this?"

"Oh no, Mrs Haas," he said without any hesitation. "That won't be possible."

His certainty felt like a slap round the face. I was devastated to think that I wasn't going to be able to take the evidence that I needed to study.

"We may be able to arrange a microfiche to be posted to you," he went on, obviously able to see my disappointment and immediately re-igniting my hopes. "Let me find out."

I had been pretty sure that he wouldn't be able to answer this himself and I was right. He scurried away to find Frau Steglitz. I knew I was pushing my luck because it was a miracle we had been allowed access to as much material as we had, but I didn't think we had anything to lose and I really needed to get those copies back to England. This forthright approach to asking for what we wanted had worked for us before, maybe it would work again. I went back to reading while I waited for him to return.

When the Director appeared beside us in the reading room she was wearing the same stern face with which she had greeted us when we had first arrived uninvited. It looked very much as if I were trying her patience by making yet more demands, when the Minister had, in her eyes, already been more than generous in his concessions. Unsure how to deal with such a request she had reverted to the same aggressive persona she had used when we first arrived unannounced on her doorstep.

"You want copies?" she asked, eyebrows arched with incredulity at my nerve in asking for so much. "Impossible."

My heart sank. Although I had surpassed all my own expectations by being allowed to delve this far into the archives, I didn't want to have to leave my search now when I was so close to finding out what had happened to Emilie and Charlotte after August's death. There was still a huge and mysterious gap in my family's history. If the documents all went back into the archives now, who knew how long it would be before I would be allowed access again, if ever?

"But Frau Steglitz, my whole life is in those files," I pleaded. "It's my history and my grandmother's history, and my children's. I could never hope to cover it all in a few days. There is so much more I haven't discovered."

"We may be able to put it onto a microfiche for you," she said, seeming to relent surprisingly quickly and reviving my optimism yet again, just as Herr Waltmann had done only minutes earlier. "We'll send it to you in England. There will of course be a charge."

I tried not to show how excited I was by this offer. I had already learned that it didn't pay to seem too thankful for anything she might do for me for fear of embarrassing her. I didn't care how much it cost. Having got this far I was willing to pay virtually anything they asked.

"Thank you," I said, as calmly as I could manage. "That's kind of you."

She gave a curt nod, accepting my thanks, and left the room while we tidied up the loose ends with Herr Waltmann. Once he had gone I picked up another file that was on the desk and began to read it, eager to use every moment we still had to its maximum advantage, and soon became absorbed once more.

"Herr Haas," a voice said from the doorway, "could you spare us a moment?"

Assuming they were going to ask him for details of where to send the microfiche or how we intended to pay, I didn't even bother to look up, and just kept reading as Ken went out to speak with whoever had called him, hungry to cover as much material as I possibly could before it was time to leave.

CHAPTER
EIGHTEEN

An Offer to Spy

After ten minutes I realised Ken hadn't come back and began to wonder what could be keeping him. I continued thumbing through the file for another ten minutes before I could contain my curiosity no longer and went to the door to see if I could find him. Just at that moment he reappeared in the corridor and came towards me, looking ashen, his face as white as a sheet.

"Where have you been?" I asked. "Are you all right?"

He said nothing, just taking me by the arm and leading me to the far corner of the room where we had been sitting. He placed his mouth close to my ear, his eyes darting round the room as if terrified of something or someone. Seeing him that badly shaken I knew it was something serious and I felt a chill of fear passing through me. Had they changed their minds about giving us the material? Or was it worse than that? Was it possible they weren't going to allow us to return to the West at all?

"I've just had a meeting with Frau Steglitz and some other man from outside the Archive," he whispered. "They've asked me to spy for them, and they want my first assignment to be in Washington, when I go there.

They say we won't have to pay anything for the microfiche if we help them. I told them I have no plans to go to Washington, but they refuse to let go. They know everything about my past; which countries I've visited, who my business contacts are, everything."

"What did they want you to get for them in Washington?" I was shocked. It was like a scene from a James Bond movie. If it hadn't been for the look on his face I would have thought he was pulling my leg.

"They want me to get them intelligence documents from the Space Center. I told them I have never had anything to do with the Space Center and that I couldn't help them because I wasn't going there. But they don't seem to even hear me. They know how much we want these copies so they think they can make any demands they want. I kept on saying 'no' to everything they asked and they just kept on ignoring me."

I might have been spending my time over the previous months trying to convince Ken that he was exaggerating when he talked about the perils we would be facing if we came to East Germany, but even I could see that we were now in considerable danger. Refusing to spy for a totalitarian state when you are inside their borders is a fearful situation to be in. Our fate was completely in their hands. If they chose to arrest us now there would be nothing we could do and no one we could turn to for protection or justice. There was no question of extending our stay now; we had to get across the border as quickly as possible. I looked up at the clock. It was three o'clock.

"We have two hours left," I said, still thinking about the files that lay unread on the table, their contents unknown to us. "Let's salvage what we can in case we don't get another chance and leave just as we planned to all along."

Pale and tight-lipped, Ken nodded in agreement and we sat down to work again as if nothing out of the ordinary had occurred. Even as I strained to follow the words I was reading, I was horribly aware of the minutes ticking away.

I tried to put everything else out of my mind in order to cram in as much reading as I possibly could before it was too late, concentrating on losing myself in the world of August and Emilie for what I feared might be the last time, desperately trying to let everything else pass me by. Ken, still visibly shaken by his experience, was trying to do the same by my side.

"Herr Haas. Frau Haas."

Two hours later an unfamiliar voice startled me and I look round to find a young lady who we had never seen before, beckoning us towards the door.

"The Director would like to invite you to take tea with her before you leave."

We exchanged nervous looks and stood up, like two naughty schoolchildren being called in by the authorities for a telling off. Was this where they were going to make it clear that they had done us a favour and it was now our turn to repay it? Or were they going to tell us that if we didn't agree to do what they wanted they would be arresting us? By accepting their hospitality so quickly were we accidentally signing a pact with the devil, which we were now going to pay for dearly? I remembered how strongly the Consul in West Berlin had advised us not to make the trip across the border, warning us that they had no diplomatic relations with the East Germans. His message had been clear enough, if we got into trouble on the other side of the border there would be nothing he could do to help us.

Neither of us spoke as we made what felt like a very long walk to the Director's office, both of us having the same thoughts and determined not to allow the fear to show in our faces. Were we going to be driving back across the border tonight or were we going to be looking at the inside of prison cells? Were they going to find a reason to keep us in the East until Ken had agreed to work for them? Would we be trapped in the hotel again, waiting forever for them to agree to give us the authorisation to leave? I was desperately trying to work out what was the most likely outcome of the meeting I was now heading for.

Walking as if we were both on our way to our executions, we followed the young woman into Frau Steglitz's office, where the Director greeted us with another of her beaming smiles, apparently delighted to see us once more. It seemed her anger at my request for copies was forgotten, and likewise Ken's refusal to spy for them. The speed with which her moods could change was unnerving. It was impossible to even guess what might truly be going on in her mind as she welcomed us in. Herr Waltmann was also in the room, looking less than comfortable to be socialising with his

175

boss, his eyes glued to the floor. There was no sign of the other man whom Ken had met; he had melted away as if he had never been there.

"Come in, come in," Frau Steglitz greeted us. "Please sit down and join us for tea. I am so glad that your research has gone so well this week."

It was like she was trying to make normal, polite tea-party conversation. An immaculate tea service had been laid out in readiness for us, including a beautiful silver teapot unlike anything I had seen anyone else being allowed to use in the building all week. Had it not been for Ken's interview with them a couple of hours before, we would have been under the impression that she considered us to be honoured guests and that she was genuinely sad to see us go and wanted to give us a good send-off, but now we knew that nothing was done in that world without an ulterior motive. Our gushing hostess poured the tea as she chatted cheerily.

"Perhaps I was not so friendly when you first came to see me," she said. "You must understand that we have not met people like you in forty years."

Determined not to say anything that might lead to another breakdown in communications between us when there was still so much information I needed to get from the archives, and when we were so anxious to get back to the safety of West Berlin, we said nothing about the offer that Ken had just been made and concentrated on returning her polite teatime conversation, playing the same game as her. As Frau Steglitz chattered away like we were old friends I found myself warming to her in a way I hadn't up till then, even though I knew I couldn't trust her and that she might turn against us again at any moment. I could more than understand how living under communism had made her the way she was when we first arrived. We had been asking her for favours that it was not within her power to grant, opening her up to possible reprimands from above. It was no wonder she had been so defensive. We had experienced the same reaction everywhere, from the border guards to the unfortunate Victor who had been spirited away from our evil influence in the hotel dining room.

The conversation at the tea party remained cordial and superficial until the end, when we finally had to say goodbye and go outside to our car in order to return to the West.

"Be under no illusions, Evi," Ken warned when we finally drove away, "we've been here long enough."

Although I was sad to be leaving August and Emilie behind after feeling I had got to know them so well, I was relieved in many ways to be heading home. Ken was right, there was always a feeling in the East that things could turn against us at any moment and we would have had no one to go to for help if we had suddenly found ourselves arrested on some trumped-up charge. Now that we knew what they were planning, I could see that Ken had been right about their friendliness, that one should always be alert, for it could be a front and a means to an end that only they knew.

The Minister had welcomed us in on the first day we arrived in their country, when Ken had been so desperately bluffing in order to hide his fears and to disguise the fact that we had no official permission to be there. Had the Minister known that he wanted to recruit Ken as a spy the day we walked into his office? It all seemed too absurd to be true. I fought to dismiss such thoughts and to keep my faith in human nature. I so much wanted things to be as I had always thought them to be. I wanted to believe that the Minister was a kind and genuine man who had had a great, great grandmother just like me; that he only had humanitarian motives for helping me. I kept raking over every detail of our interview with him in my mind. The authorities had had time to check us out after receiving our first letter requesting access to the archives. Had they already known everything about Ken's business at that stage?

Now I had some time to think about it, I could see that it was possible that the whole day could have been orchestrated by them. Did Frau Steglitz, or someone more senior to whom she had reported, contact the Minister when we arrived at Merseburg, and did he then instruct her to give us his address? That would explain why she suddenly produced it after seeming so unhelpful a few minutes before. No, I tried to convince myself, she threw us out because we were bothering her, that's how it had felt at any rate. But she did warn us that it was forbidden to go to Potsdam, so why then did she give us the address of the Ministry? Then there was the helicopter that tracked us along the autobahn. At that stage they may have suspected that we were spies ourselves and that the whole story about my family was just an invented excuse to get into their archives. Ken had said at the time that he didn't trust the Minister and didn't believe any of his promises. I couldn't accept that the Minister had been reeling us in from the start. I still believed that he genuinely wanted to help us, because I so much wanted that to be the truth. But was it?

What was certain, was that the authorities had allowed us to see enough of the material early on in our visit to make sure we would be desperate for more, before putting their offer on the table at the very moment when they knew how desperate I was for copies. If they were listening in to our conversations at the hotel as well they would have known exactly how badly I needed to complete my research and how much Ken was willing to put himself out in order to help me get what I wanted. They had left it until the very last moment to spring their trap. Right then there was no point in trying to work it all out. Our first priority had to be to make sure we got back to the West safely.

The border we were heading for this time was in a place called Drewitz, outside Berlin. As we approached, the East German guard waved us away from the other cars and indicated we should stop. It looked like he had been expecting us and my heartbeat quickened uncomfortably. I took some deep breaths, willing myself to stay calm.

"*Austeigen!*" ("Get out!") he yelled angrily.

We obeyed and several other guards started checking the car from end to end, working their way methodically through what looked like a well-rehearsed routine without saying another word to us. We might as

179

well have been invisible, or at the very least unworthy of their consideration. The original man who had pulled us over stood with us, staring all the time with no expression on his face, perhaps hoping we would crack and confess to stealing something from the archive or give a sign that would indicate they were close to finding what they were looking for in the car. I could feel my heart still thumping, not because I had a guilty conscience, as we didn't even have Victor's promised salami let alone any stolen papers, but because I was terrified they would find something we knew nothing about. You never know what someone else might have planted on you in a situation like that. The guards appeared so certain that we were trying to hide something it seemed possible they had been tipped off, but whatever it was we knew nothing about it.

What if the authorities had decided they wanted to keep us in the country? It was quite possible that something of value from the archive could have been planted in our car. They would have had plenty of time to do whatever they wanted while we were absorbed in our work in the reading room, or taking tea with Frau Steglitz. Maybe that was what the whole tea-party charade had been about, a way of ensuring that we did not go back to the car until they had planted whatever they wanted us to be arrested for. My head was spinning now as I tried to work out what might be about to happen. If they arrested us for spying or stealing they could slap us straight into jail and we would have virtually no chance of proving our innocence. The Consul in West Berlin had made it very clear that there would be nothing Britain could do to help us if things went wrong on this side of the Wall.

Maybe, I told myself, there was no sinister plot. Maybe they were simply worried we were trying to smuggle out some of the papers from the archive since they knew how much I wanted them. Probably Frau Steglitz had phoned ahead and told them to check, just in case. Once they realised that we had nothing they would have to let us pass. We just had to hold our nerve until the search was over. I glanced at Ken and although he was pale he was managing to look completely impassive. Apparently satisfied that the car was clean, the guards then turned their attentions to us.

"Open your handbag," one of them ordered me. I did as he told me and passed it over. He rummaged carelessly around inside and pulled out a photograph. "What's that?" he demanded.

"It's an old picture of my mother," I fired back, staring right into his face. My anger was rising at their rudeness and the invasion of my privacy; a little of my self-confidence was starting to ebb back.

Eventually satisfied that we hadn't stolen anything they begrudgingly ordered us back into the car and waved us through. Ken and I exchanged a relieved glance as we drove slowly forward. It seemed we were safe, at least for the moment. Although I still had a long way to go in my quest, I felt a strange sense of euphoria as we passed the West German guards at the thought of how much we had managed to achieve over the previous few weeks in the face of the odds stacked against us.

The following day, after a long night's sleep, we flew back to England, bursting with excitement at the thought of sharing everything we had learned with the boys. When we finally walked through our front door in Highgate it felt very good to be home, however much I might have wanted to stay on in that reading room in Merseburg until I had extracted every possible drop of information. Now all I had to do was wait patiently to see if the microfiches turned up.

I had played this waiting game before and I knew just how hard on the nerves it could be, but it was a lot better than being locked up in an East German prison. I felt that I was finally getting closer to Anna. I had promised I would never forget her and I felt so uplifted that I had gone to such lengths to prove it. I tried to shut Emilie and August and Charlotte out of my mind for a while and think of other things, but it was impossible. I had become so determined to find out what had happened to them and I knew in my heart that if the microfiche didn't arrive I would have to think of another way to uncover the truth and get to the answers that I needed.

CHAPTER
NINETEEN

Calling Their Bluff

After ten days of watching the post and pretending not to be disappointed every time it brought nothing from Merseburg, an envelope materialised from the archive in just the same way as the permission to travel there had arrived from the Minister. Picking it up off the mat with trepidation I gave it a surreptitious squeeze in the hope that there might be a microfiche inside, but even before I opened it I knew that it was just a letter with no enclosures. Ken was standing beside me as I carefully slit the envelope open, nervous of damaging the contents, unfolded the letter and read it out loud.

> *Your two hundred and seventy-five documents are now ready, and they will be forwarded to you immediately on receipt of the documents from Washington.*

There was no invoice. I didn't know whether to laugh at the ludicrousness of their attempt to recruit Ken for their impossible mission, or to cry at my disappointment at yet another delay in finding out what had happened to my ancestors. It seemed they had decided to ignore Ken's refusal to be recruited and go to Washington on their secret mission, and intended to continue as if it were all going ahead. Perhaps they believed that we would be unable to resist the offer of the information and that once we had received it Ken would then be in their power, obligated to do whatever they asked of him.

"This could spell disaster," I said once I'd had a few minutes for the importance of it to sink in. "They're trying to trap us, Ken. We have to report it. We should go at once to the Foreign Office and explain what has happened."

Everyone in authority in those days took the communist threat to the western way of life very seriously. At that time the Soviet Empire was perceived to be a superpower and no one ever imagined that the whole façade would crumble away to nothing 15 years later. There were still stories appearing in the papers all the time about agents being murdered all over the world, and John le Carré's bestselling spy novels were believed to be an accurate picture of the espionage world of the time. Just because we were back in London wouldn't mean that we were beyond their reach should they decide to come looking for us.

The western governments of the time took all intelligence matters to do with Eastern Europe far more seriously than they do today. The communists were seen then in the same light as terrorists are now. So we had no trouble persuading the person at the

Foreign Office who took our call to make an appointment for us to come in for a meeting immediately. In fact, we found ourselves in Whitehall the very next morning. The man we were taken to meet towered over us as he came out to shake hands. I noticed he had the biggest feet and the longest fingers I have ever seen. I would say he was in his mid forties. He introduced himself as James Howard.

"I'm Head of Station," he said, once we were sitting down in his office. "Tell me what I can do for you."

I unravelled our story for him as best I could. There was so much to tell and as I talked I wondered whether my words sounded believable. He listened with rapt attention, absent-mindedly tapping a pencil on his desk as tea was brought in.

Mr Howard shook his head as I reached the climax of the story. "They are very naughty," he said when I finally finished and pulled out the letter we had received the day before. It was as if he were talking about a bunch of schoolboys who had been caught smoking behind the bike sheds. "This is no way to behave. You have been put in danger and in an impossible position. As you know we have no diplomatic relations with East Germany so we have to handle things a bit delicately. Do you still need these documents, and do you want to maintain your relationship with the people at the archives?"

"Oh, yes," I said, very quickly. "I most certainly do. I need those documents, I really do, and I must be able to talk to Herr Waltmann on the phone whenever I need to check something. It will be a complete disaster if I lose my access to them."

He nodded his understanding. "Leave it to us," he said. "Don't worry, we'll fix it for you."

We said a big thank you to the Spymaster and took our leave.

"Ken, I am impressed," I admitted once we were outside. "Should I be? How could they possibly fix it? The East Germans are under no obligation at all. They can deny that the documents even exist, can't they?"

"These people know exactly what to do, Evi," he assured me.

"But, we don't have any diplomatic relations."

"We have to wait, let them do their work," he said. "It's the waiting game again."

I was relieved to have the Foreign Office involved. I had felt very vulnerable when we had been on the other side of the border, basically on our own, and I didn't want to be looking over my shoulder the whole time in London. Now I felt that we had some protection, although I couldn't see how the Foreign Office were going to be able to have much effect if there was no diplomatic contact between the two countries. I had a horrible feeling I was never going to hear another word from Frau Steglitz or Herr Waltmann and that my researches might now have come to an end.

We went home, not knowing what was going to happen next, sifting eagerly through the post each morning and going away disappointed yet again. After three weeks, however, another letter with an East German stamp arrived. I opened it and held my breath.

It was short and to the point, and there was an invoice attached for around three hundred pounds. I read the brief letter over and over to ensure I had understood it.

On receipt of your payment we shall send your documents.

"Ken, Ken, we've done it," I shouted. "Our man at the Ministry is a magician."

I ran to find Ken, waving the letter excitedly, bumping into Timothy and throwing my arms around him and jumping up and down in my excitement. "They somehow managed it."

Three hundred pounds was an awful lot of money in those days, but if it produced the documents it would be worth every penny. In order to send money to East Germany we had to make special arrangements in person with our bank, so we headed off into Hampstead the same day. That night we talked of nothing else, wondering now if we had lost our money, since there would have been no way we could have chased it up if they had simply denied receiving it.

But fate was on our side once more. The crucial evidence that Ken and I had gathered together in East Germany, the microfiche with all of the 275 documents that we had selected, plopped through the letterbox as promised ten days later. As if by magic, all that I had hoped and prayed for was literally delivered to our doorstep. This time we actually went out and bought a bottle of champagne to celebrate. I was ecstatic. Now I could spend as long as I needed studying the papers in my search for the answers and I could take the evidence to show to the network of historians and experts I had built up in the West since my search first began. Most important of all, the microfiche that arrived that day served to spur me on, to make me even more determined than ever to find the missing piece of the jigsaw. I was sure that whatever had happened to Emilie and Charlotte after the King's refusal to allow Emilie to keep the title "Frau", could help to explain why Granny Anna met the fate she did.

CHAPTER
TWENTY

The Prince in England

Over the following years there was seldom a moment when I wasn't thinking about the stories of August, Emilie, Charlotte and Anna, turning over all the possibilities in my head, trying out different theories and speculations, trying to merge guesswork with the basic historical facts that I had been able to put together so far. I had always been curious about my family's past, but I had never anticipated how completely the hunt for the truth would take over my thoughts. During the long weeks of waiting for the microfiches I had been making new contacts wherever I could, ringing and Writing to museums, archives, antiquarian booksellers and anyone else I could think of who just might have something in their files that would shed even the tiniest shard of light on the mysteries surrounding my ancestors. All of these paths were leading to dead ends, just as they always had, despite the fact that I managed to infect many of my newfound contacts with my own obsessions and they would go well beyond the call of duty in their attempts to help me.

I thought about my Granny Anna: she was my reason for embarking on this incredible journey of discovery. How clever it was of her, and so selfless, so typical, to hand the small pocket-book over to my father when she did in 1932, just before she left Berlin for Czechoslovakia, because it was through that one small action that the book had ended up in my hands. So far I had managed to find my way round the obstructive East German bureaucracy and past the wishes of an all-powerful nineteenth-century Prussian monarch in order to dig up facts that they had all wanted buried, so I wasn't about to give up now, no matter how many new obstacles were placed in my path or how discouraged I might feel some days.

"I just want to uncover the truth," I would tell Ken whenever he questioned the amount of time I was dedicating to the search. But I still couldn't find out what had happened to Emilie after August's death. And their daughter, Charlotte, seemed to be completely invisible. I needed to know how it was that my grandmother, Anna, who was the granddaughter of a Prussian prince, could have died as a Jew when all the time her grandmother was, it now transpired, a Polish aristocrat and her mother the daughter of a prince. How could she be Jewish if her mother and grandmother were not? I had no wish to acquire any new status or to enrich myself in any way by discovering the secrets of my past, I just wanted to know the truth.

Even though we had come so far, resolving the last remaining piece of the puzzle was an uphill struggle. I didn't know where to go or what to do in order to find the answers that I needed. I did realise, however, that returning to Merseburg was out of the question. Maybe that was why my mother and father warned me not to try to find out anything; maybe they realised that if I once set off down that path I would become too involved and might well end up bitterly disappointed. Well, that I certainly wasn't, for I had found Emilie and her life with August, but I desperately wanted to find the last few pieces of the jigsaw.

Back in England I requested permission to search in the Queen's private archive at Windsor Castle and was graciously given as much access as I needed. There I discovered that August had been a friend of the Duke of Wellington (the Iron Duke), and I found a book of letters from Princess Charlotte, who was the youngest daughter of the Prince Regent (the son of George III), edited in 1949 by Professor Arthur Aspinall. The Princess wrote about how August had been invited to London with King Frederick William III in 1814 to attend the victory celebrations a year after he had defeated Napoleon at Leipzig. (They didn't realise that as they celebrated, Napoleon was already hatching his plan to escape from captivity in Elba.)

The papers of the time wrote of how the Prince was revered by the British for his bravery and for masterminding Napoleon's downfall as Inspector General and Head of the Prussian Artillery. In letters from Wellington to August, which I found at Southampton University, the Duke marvelled at the loyalty August had inspired in his troops, asking him how he managed it. Although sadly I have not been able to trace August's reply, it was well documented how much he cared about his men and how well he looked after them. They responded to this attitude by giving him their undying loyalty. Whenever he went into battle he always led from the front, putting himself directly in the firing line. He was an heroic figure in every sense of the word, exactly the sort of leader who can inspire other people to achieve great things.

The Iron Duke also visited Berlin to meet August again on his way to the Tsar of Russia's funeral, after the Napoleonic wars had ended.

While he was in London the 36-year-old August took part in the grand parade staged to celebrate the defeat of Napoleon and the return of the French royal family from London to Paris after the Revolution. He also took part in a salute for the Tsar of Russia in Hyde Park. He would have been dressed with all his usual splendour for such occasions and his dashing figure was spotted by Princess Charlotte, who was eighteen at the time and the Prince Regent's heir apparent. In one letter the Princess wrote that she thought him by far the most impressive-looking man amongst the many leaders gathered there to accept the glory of a great victory.

Since this was a girl who, after her father the Prince Regent, would become the Queen of England, she was not free to love whoever she chose. Her father, who could make her do almost anything he wished, wanted her to marry William of Orange, the heir to the throne of Holland. It was a match that Charlotte herself was not happy about. This celebrated young Prussian Prince looked much more like her ideal man.

At a state dinner thrown by the Prince Regent at Carlton House, the Princess was determined to make an impression on the glamorous Prussian war hero and appeared in what was described in the records as a "shimmering" dress. August, not surprisingly, was unable to resist the temptation and the couple began a short, clandestine affair. Charlotte lived in Warwick House, which was right next door to Carlton House. The two of them quietly sidled out of the banqueting hall and conducted their affair in the privacy and comfort of her boudoir. He was at the time separated from his first wife and things became so intense between him and Charlotte that he even promised to marry her as soon as he was able. By reading their private correspondence I was left in no doubt about their mutual infatuation.

I discovered that when Charlotte's father, the Prince Regent, found out about the affair August had to leave England immediately to avoid a scandal. He returned home where the King appointed him as his representative to negotiate on his behalf at the Congress of Vienna. All the sovereigns and diplomats in Europe were meeting there to try to agree on the future frontiers of Europe, just as Napoleon landed at Golfe Juan having escaped from Elba. While he was there Princess Charlotte wrote that she was certain he would return to Britain and ask Parliament to allow him to marry her. The Prince, on the other hand, with no official duties in the city, was taking advantage of the endless round of society balls and festivities that were happening all over Vienna and did not hurry back to London as he had apparently promised the Princess he would, quite possibly because the girl's father had expressed his obvious disapproval of the match. When he failed to return as she expected Princess Charlotte was broken-hearted.

The English Princess must have been considered a loose cannon by the British Establishment because she was put under house arrest by her unkind father until she agreed to give up all hope of marrying Prince August and agreed instead to make a marriage that was considered advantageous to the royal family. It wasn't long before Charlotte married Prince Leopold of Sachsen-Coburg, a Russian general who would later become King of the Belgians, and it seems unlikely that it was a love match. As if her story wasn't sad enough, she died soon afterwards in the process of giving birth to a stillborn child. Life could be hard for even the most well-born and privileged women in those times. The more I read the more clearly I could picture my swashbuckling and famous great, great grandfather, and the more sympathy I felt for the many women in the family who had been forced to live in his considerable shadow, particularly Emilie.

CHAPTER
TWENTY-ONE

Visiting August

By now I was feeling as if I were as deeply within Prince August's thrall as the women who knew him when he was alive. Everything about him was fascinating and I was always hungry for more information and more details about his life. I wanted to visit August's birthplace, which was his father's summer palace in Friedrichsfelde. I had read in the archives about how the usual tranquillity of the palace had been shattered on 26 September 1779 by the christening party thrown for the baby son of Prince Ferdinand and his wife, Princess Anna Elisabeth Louise and wanted to see it for myself.

Despite the fact that Prince August was the royal couple's sixth child, it was inevitable that it would be a grand event. Prince Ferdinand was the younger brother of the King, while his wife was the King's niece. His Majesty King Friedrich II, Europe's most famous monarch at the time and better known in history as "Frederick the Great", arrived from Sanssoucci Palace in Potsdam, for the christening of August, a baby who was destined to become his favourite nephew, riding in his old-fashioned, silver-trimmed coach, drawn by eight horses. The rest of the royal family were already assembled there and waiting for him, including his Queen (who remained enormously loyal to him throughout her life, despite the fact that she hardly ever saw him), and the young wife of the heir to the Russian throne, who was also a niece of August's proud mother.

It must have been a glorious sight to have so many powerful and wealthy European titles in one place, so many of them interlinked by propitious marriages and a network of family ties. The ceremony started and the newest addition to the family was formally presented to the King, his uncle. August would spend his first five summers and autumns at this palace with his brothers and sisters, until their parents moved to the newly built Bellevue Palace and I was curious to see the place that would have had such a formative effect on the person he became.

It was 1985 by the time I finally arrived at the palace, over 200 years after August had lived there. My years of research meant that I came armed with an enormous fund of knowledge about the life that lay ahead of the tiny baby who had been at the centre of that christening, and the small child who had subsequently played in the surrounding gardens. By 1985 the bad feelings of the Cold War were starting to improve, but it was still a frightening thought for Ken and me to return to the East and risk rekindling the whole spying affair, even though more than twelve years had passed since our time in Merseburg. We told ourselves that it was such a long while ago it must now be safe, and it had happened at the height of the Cold War. We made what we felt was a practical decision, and brushed any negative thoughts away.

This time we took the train, called the S-Bahn, which delivered us to Friedrichstrasse, the border station. There we stepped out and met the border guards again. Past experiences had left their mark on me and I couldn't help feeling nervous. By that time the situation between East and West was very different. We had been told that a thaw had set in, so it should have felt less threatening. Nevertheless those dark memories we had carried over the years still haunted us and it took all of my self-control not to show how they were stirring up our old fears with their angry voices and cold eyes. We obeyed their orders without question. I was taken into one room by an interrogator while Ken was told to remain outside. I didn't like being parted from him at all, but I didn't want to cause any trouble. To my horror I heard the lock on the door click behind me as I went in. So, this was the result of thawing relations?

Why did they feel the need to lock me in when firing questions at me, unless it was simply to intimidate me? Forcing myself to keep calm I sat, as instructed, and answered questions as politely as I could for what seemed like an age. My interrogator wanted to know all about my life, asking searching and intrusive questions about what I planned to do in East Germany that day. My biggest worry was that he would contact someone who would know that Ken had refused to spy for them on our last visit, and that we were on a list somewhere. I tried to quell my fears but my interrogator was not letting up, so maybe he already knew about us. My imagination was running riot and I was expecting him to start throwing accusations at me at any moment.

Eventually he seemed to back off and didn't appear to make any connection to our past visits. I came out through another exit and Ken was then led in to the room and interrogated behind the same locked doors. After twenty-five minutes we were told we could continue on our journey. As we left, Ken explained that despite everything that had happened their policy was still one of intimidation and fear as we took the U-Bahn, a tube train, to our final destination outside Berlin, Friedrichsfelde.

We walked down a long driveway to reach the palace where August had been born, and as we walked I imagined Frederick the Great riding along this very road in his silver coach to join the christening party. We had no idea what we would find once we went inside the palace.

A small boy was walking with his father in front of us. "Who lives behind that wall, Papa?" he asked, pointing to a high wall that separated August's old home from the house next door.

"Only idiots, my son," the man spat contemptuously. "Idiots are living in there."

The East German State, it transpired, had turned the neighbouring property into a mental institution.

Eventually realising that they had a place of historical interest on their hands, the authorities had started arranging for guided tours of the former palace and we duly joined one that was about to be taken inside. The guide was a woman who talked confidently about the history of the house, but when she mentioned the names of the many previous occupants, neither Prince August nor his family were among them. I couldn't work out whether I thought she was rewriting history under official instruction or if she really didn't know that they had lived there. I kept quiet until we got upstairs and I managed to get her on her own.

"Which room did Prince Ferdinand, Frederick the Great's brother, use as his office?" I asked innocently. "And do you know where in the house Prince August was born?"

The poor woman looked panic-stricken for a moment at being asked something unexpected, and then obviously decided there was no option but to come clean.

"Yes, of course," she said, "Prince August and his family also lived here too."

She then moved on quickly before I could cross-examine her as to why she had not thought such facts important enough to mention during the tour. We had come all this way to visit August's family's former home, only to find that the East German establishment still wanted to forget that Prince August had ever existed. It seemed there would never be an end to the layers of mystery surrounding the family. Much later I discovered that a similar historical cull had happened at the palace in Prillvitz where Emilie spent much of her time. The building became a hotel and my son, Timothy, called the owner to find out if he knew anything about the family's connection to the building. The owner was thrilled to hear about our family story, because he said, "part of the history of this house is a complete mystery to us." He encouraged Timothy to tell him everything he knew.

"There is a complete blank," he explained when Timothy had finished, "between the years of 1820 and 1845. There are no records of Prince August having lived here or what went on. I just don't understand it because usually records in these parts are detailed and well documented, unless the bombing in the war destroyed them, which is not the case here."

When Ken and I were on our way back from the house at Friedrichsfelde we decided the time had finally come for us to visit August himself. To do that we needed to go to the Dome, a cathedral in East Berlin that housed the bodies of the Prussian kings and many other senior members of the Hohenzollern family. It required us to make a special detour and throughout the journey I felt a range of emotions creeping up on me. August's funeral was foremost in my mind, with images of Emilie having to watch from the sidelines pervading my thoughts again. Travelling around the Eastern Bloc still served as a constant reminder to us how lucky we were to enjoy the freedoms that we took for granted in England, the country that came to the rescue of my family when we faced such a disastrous future in Germany all those years ago.

The Dome was exactly as I had imagined it to be, a majestic and beautifully rounded building befitting the status it had acquired as the final resting place for Prussia's elite. We discovered that it was being restored and that the coffins of the Prussian kings and their families were on display where they had been safely preserved for so many years.

Standing there, next to the man who had had such a profound effect on my life, was spine-chilling. Nearly fifty years had passed since my father had given me his pocket-book to hold in my hands, and now here I was right next to him, running my hand over what seemed like a well-fashioned oak surface. Inside the coffin was the man who had been part of so many historical events and had influenced so many people's lives, in Prussia and in Europe during one of its most tumultuous periods: August the defender, who refused to give in to Napoleon's conquering ambitions. It seemed like the scandal of August's last years with Emilie had consigned him to the dustbin of history for over a century but now my rediscovery of his life meant that history itself had to be in part rewritten to include events that had been so carefully tucked away from prying eyes by the royal establishment and then the communists.

We had read that August had stipulated that he wanted nothing extravagant when he died, that his coffin should be "plain and fashioned from ordinary wood". Despite this stipulation it still looked very substantial. There was a golden crown placed at the head, but otherwise it was not overly decorated or showy like the ones belonging to other family members. To be standing so close to this man I felt I had grown to know so much about produced an intense feeling in me. It was like visiting a dear friend after a long separation.

CHAPTER
TWENTY-TWO

An Ally in Berlin

Although I hadn't much taken to the director of the Dahlem archive in West Berlin when I had gone there at the start of my quest in 1973, I decided to go back there a few years later with some of the documents that I now had in my possession. I thought that if I could show him that it was possible to find material, even if it was buried behind the Iron Curtain, it might inspire him to dig a little deeper in his own files. To my delight I discovered when I arrived that the director I had met previously had retired and been replaced by a gentle man called Dr Eckart Henning, who responded to my story with all the amazement and enthusiasm I could have hoped for as I showed him what I had found so far.

"I think they must have a love affair with you to give you access to all this," he laughed as I spread copies of some of the documents before him. "This is unheard of; we have no record of them doing this for anyone before. Do you have any idea how many Americans come over trying to prove they have a connection to the Royal Hohenzollern family, hoping to get some of the status and perhaps even some of the money? They all get turned away at the door, but you they have invited in to their parlour. Do you know anything about the legacy of August's grandfather, Frederick William I?"

"A little," I replied.

"Well, Prince August had agreed not to leave any legitimate heirs. At the end of his life much of his wealth was returned to the Crown. It was a stipulation in Frederick William I's original will that the legacy August received could only be inherited by those who left legitimate heirs. After the will was disputed by the King, August agreed not to leave any legitimate heirs."

"I assume you know that we do have some papers here on the Gottschalk family and Prince August," he asked. "They were apparently hidden in a drawer. We do not know by whom."

"No," I said, feeling even more bewildered. Was there no end to the layers of historical subterfuge that my poor family had been subjected to? "Your predecessor told us there was nothing here about Prince August, and certainly not about the Gottschalks. In fact he told me he had never heard of the name. Why would he say that if it wasn't true?"

"I have no idea but I will arrange for you to see these papers," Dr Henning said helpfully. "Please come with me, I'll fetch them now."

He made a call and a few minutes later led Ken and me to a private room, where we found a set of papers laid out before us on a table.

"These are all we have on the Prince August," he explained before leaving Ken and me to go back to our studies, just as we had done in Merseburg, as hungry as ever for new information.

"This is extraordinary," I said after a few minutes, waving a piece of paper in the air. "It's Isadore Gottschalk, August's tailor again. According to this he sued August in the 1820s. His daughter, Friederike Gottschalk, is accusing August of seducing her. She claims she was visiting the Prince to collect a debt owed to her cousin, Goldman, who was an actor. Apparently Louis Ferdinand, August's brother, borrowed money from the actor just before he was killed at Saalfield in 1806. Friederike went to the Bellevue Palace to see the Prince for settlement of his late brother's debt. It seems her father, Isadore Gottschalk, had been thrown into a debtor's prison and she needed the money in order to secure a release."

If a man as well born and wealthy as Louis Ferdinand had borrowed money from a humble actor, that would suggest that Louis Ferdinand was leading a fairly dissolute life. In his own defence August denied completely the Gottschalk girl's accusation that he had forced himself on her at the meeting, and as evidence in his defence he was able to prove that she had returned next day for a second visit. He claimed that when she came to him, imploring him to honour his late brother's debt so she had the money to set her father free, he had told her to come back the next day to receive some money. He claimed that she then framed him and accused him of seduction in order to create a scandal and fleece him of a great deal more money than his brother's original debt. If that was the case then the girl's plan worked perfectly because, according to the file now in front of me, although the allegation was unproven the King still commanded August to settle his brother's outstanding debt and to pay a further sum in order to avoid the scandal getting more out of control. Given the Prince's vulnerable social standing and his attraction to the young ladies of Berlin, it is understandable that he was easy prey for such allegations and that the Gottschalk girl might have seen an opportunity to extract money from a man who was well known for his love of life.

Friederike Gottschalk went on to give birth to a daughter who she claimed was the product of the alleged seduction, a mentally handicapped girl called Agnes. August was not willing to accept that the child was his without a fight and his spies found out that at the same time she was paying him the two visits, she was also frequenting the nearby army camps in the area and it was said that she had been sleeping around with the soldiers. It was a story that would have delighted the tabloid editors of today.

August never admitted anything, but there was a record of his making financial provision for Agnes to be looked after for the whole of her life. It would not be unheard of for someone like the Prince to help out a man like Isadore Gottschalk out of the goodness of his heart, even if he didn't have a guilty conscience. The fact was that setting aside the accusations, which would have infuriated August, it was clear to him that his old tailor was in dire financial straits since he was in a debtors' prison. It would have been obvious that

Isadore couldn't possibly afford to pay for the upbringing of his daughter's disabled child. August may simply have felt sorry for him.

This new information was making me even more confused. If the Gottschalks had been angry enough at August to level such accusations at him, how did Emilie's daughter end up bearing their name? We were gathering more and more pieces to the jigsaw, but still none of them seemed to fit together to create a coherent picture of what might have happened.

CHAPTER
TWENTY-THREE

A Poisonous Legacy

Despite all the help we were receiving from Dr Henning we were still none the wiser about Charlotte and, as had happened before, the relationship between the Prince and his tailor's family appeared to be far more complicated than we could ever have imagined. It sometimes felt like every time we took one step forward we then had to take two back. My spirits would soar with every new bit of information that came my way, and then I would meet another brick wall.

While we were in Berlin I had been wracking my brains to think where I might be able to find out more about what happened to Emilie and Charlotte in 1843, after August died. It was such a crucial time for all of them I was determined to find out more about it. So we went on to another archive to look through the city's address books from the nineteenth century, these were the precursors of modern-day telephone books. We were nonchalantly turning the pages, not really sure what we were looking for when a name leaped off the page at us. To my astonishment, listed there for all to see was Emilie, in her married name as "Frau" (Mrs), von Ostrowska, just as she had described herself in her letter to the King. August had boldly decided that the whole world could know that she was married to him.

This must have been known and addressed during their married years together, just as she had told the King in her letter. Then, tense with excitement, I checked the next edition of the address book, published after August had died. Emilie's listing was there again, but this time a change had been made. The effect of the Wittgenstein reply to her letter had taken hold. Emilie was now being listed as "Fraulein" (Miss), and in those four letters her link to August was officially erased forever. Her new status as an unmarried woman with a child was stark and the ramifications would have been very frightening. Not only would this change have been humiliating, it would have meant that Emilie's world was falling apart. The change had been made and she would have no choice but to accept the consequences. The King's wishes had been carried out and Emilie, stripped of her married status, must have found her position impossible.

That would have been the same year that Charlotte told my father and uncle everything in her life "changed completely". It was hard to believe that any mother would voluntarily give up her only child, especially when she had just been widowed and must have been feeling very alone and vulnerable. So did that mean the establishment had put pressure on her to give the child away, just as callously as they had taken away her married status?

Whatever the reasons, it seemed that just after losing her husband, her father and her trusted friend, August's secretary Uhde, Emilie must also have lost her only daughter and her last connection to her beloved husband and partner of eleven years. If that was what happened, then the cruelty of it was unbearable to even think about.

I was still having trouble working out what all this would have meant as far as my great grandmother, Charlotte, was concerned. Had August secretly hoped to legitimise his descendants by marrying Emilie? Would that have been why the King was angry with them both?

"My great grandmother just doesn't seem to exist in the records," I kept explaining to anyone who would listen. "All we know is that for some reason she was given the name of this Jewish family, Gottschalk, when in fact she was a Hohenzollern princess."

As soon as we got back to London we returned once more to studying the documents on the microfiches that Frau Steglitz had sent us, searching for clues that we might now be able to spot, armed with the new information we had unearthed in Berlin. I was still having trouble working out the financial situation within the Hohenzollern family but I was coming to believe that it would prove to be crucial to solving the mystery. Dr Henning had explained the whole thing to me in principle, but then I uncovered some letters in an archive which gave an account of an event that had occurred before any of August's marriages at the turn of the century.

Reading the papers I realised that August's mother, Princess Ferdinand, had unwittingly caused a problem for her son after Prince Heinrich died and left most of his private assets to his favourite, August's brother Louis Ferdinand. Their mother had always been scathing about the louche lifestyle of Louis Ferdinand, and was horrified at the thought of him coming into yet another huge fortune without sharing it with August. So she took the matter to the King, asking him to intervene in order to ensure that August received a fair share of this inheritance.

Princess Ferdinand had always adored August to the detriment of her two other sons, even reputedly having him sleep in her room with her when he was a boy. Many believed that it had been her preference for him that had given him his over-developed sense of self-esteem and his famous obstinacy. When she was later told of Louis Ferdinand's death his mother's first words were reported as being, "Thank God it wasn't August."

The King at that stage was the financially neglected Frederick William III who, although two generations down from August, was actually nine years older than the Prince. When August's mother went to see him, requesting that he intervene on August's behalf to share the money equally between the two brothers, his Majesty's advisers looked into the detail of Frederick William I's original bequest to his sons, Heinrich and Ferdinand (August's father). Only then, apparently, did they realise that the original inheritance consisted of Crown properties and many other assets, which should have gone to their other brother, Frederick the Great, who was the new king at the time. As a result of the

211

Princess's drawing their attention to this, the entire bequest then fell into dispute, not at all the result she had hoped to achieve. Apparently alarmed by the scale of the wealth that had built up there, and wanting to ensure that as much of this valuable inheritance as possible remained with the Crown, the King came back to Princess Ferdinand with an ultimatum. He insisted that the two brothers (August and Louis Ferdinand) signed an agreement which would prevent them from leaving legitimate heirs. That would mean that all the disputed assets that were now in the hands of their father Ferdinand would be returned to the Crown once both his sons had died.

The Princess had made a grave error of judgment by bringing the matter to the attention of the King, not having imagined for a second that he would rake up something from so far in the past and try and seize the inheritance for himself. She must have been shocked at the result of her own actions. Had she simply bided her time until Louis Ferdinand's death, the entire legacy of Frederick William I, a huge fortune, would have ended up with her favourite son's heirs instead of the bulk of it having to go back to the Crown upon his death. I would imagine August and his brother must have been furious with her at the time for her interference, but it was too late for them to do anything about it.

This whole financial situation must have added to the paranoia that the King and his advisers felt towards Emilie, fearing that if the young widow actually took her case to the lawyers her daughter, Charlotte, might well end up with a claim to the Crown's vast fortunes, as well as on the eventual succession, particularly if she bore a male heir. It was extraordinary to think that so much rested on the shoulders of one tiny innocent baby girl. She could have had no idea how many generations of jealousy and ill-feeling between different branches of her famous family stretched back behind her.

So it was that much of the huge fortune that had been kept from Frederick the Great by his father (probably because he disapproved of his son's homosexuality), finally ended up with August, the supreme irony being that because of his mother's intervention none of his heirs would benefit.

I had already read about how badly Frederick the Great was treated by his tyrannical father, almost like a slave. It was no wonder, with such a terrible family history, that August had been nervous about what Wittgenstein might do to his bride. I knew August would have been the conservative Wittgenstein's worst nightmare. The Prince was wealthy, directly in line to the throne, popular with the army which had prospered under his modernisation, and extremely liberal in his views compared to the King and his close advisors. August's championing of the Jews horrified Wittgenstein who was constantly fighting to maintain the iron grip of conservatism on Prussia.

My head had been whirling as I tried to take in all the machinations of this complicated family from which I now knew I had sprung. So many names and so many generations all intermingling, it was hard to get a clear picture beyond the fact that by the time the money reached August it was a massive fortune, far bigger than the one controlled by the King himself. In those times money meant power, even more directly than it does today, which often led to bitter rivalries springing up within wealthy families and meant that thrones were always vulnerable.

One thing was crystal clear to me at this point. With August's death, Emilie's and, even more Charlotte's, lives were in peril. There had already, it seemed, been a serious attempt on Emilie's life and the possibility that Charlotte as a direct descendant of Frederick the Great had a legitimate claim to the Hohenzollern family fortune — and without August her father to protect her — now made her disappearance from historical records an almost foregone conclusion.

But the burning question for me now was: what had happened to Emilie and Charlotte?

CHAPTER
TWENTY-FOUR

Finding Charlotte

As the leads kept on piling up Ken and I were going back to Berlin on a regular basis in our continued search for any possible scraps of information about what had happened to Charlotte. I had found her marriage certificate amongst my father's papers when I first set out on my search. She had married a man called Sigmund Baumann, who my Uncle Freddy told me had been her next-door neighbour in Berlin. But I still desperately wanted to find her grave and any information at all about her birth. It seemed likely that she was born at Prillwitz, because that was where the archives told me Emilie had been staying at the time when I believed Charlotte was born, so I had hoped to be able to find the registration of the birth in that area. But when I contacted the local records office they had no record of either Charlotte von Ostrowska or Charlotte Gottschalk.

Given that we knew more about Charlotte at the end of her life than the beginning, I believed I stood a better chance of finding her grave if I just searched for long enough. But there had been two world wars in Europe since her death, and enormous social upheavals, particularly for any family that was believed to be of Jewish descent, so even that was going to be a challenge.

I knew about the big Jewish cemetery in Weissensee, a suburb of East Berlin, and we decided to look to see if by any chance Charlotte was buried there. This time we crossed the border in a taxi with no problems. I half expected to be met by yet another dead end once we got there. It was the mid-1980s by the time Ken and I got there and when I saw the size of the place my heart sank. The graves seemed to stretch to every horizon, it was a far bigger area than I could ever have imagined. We went to see the director of the cemetery and managed to convey the importance of our quest.

"We have many thousands of grave names," she admitted as she hauled out the records books, "but I will try and find her for you."

I gave her the name of Charlotte's husband, Sigmund Baumann, as it was likely the entry would be in his family name, and the dates of her life from 1838 to 1906. I was pretty sure that she had been born in 1838 because of notes that August had left and because of his concerned instructions regarding his young wife while she was at Prillwitz that year. I looked over the woman's shoulder as she searched through the book. Like so many things German, everything appeared efficiently documented and laid out.

It didn't take long at all, in fact not more than ten minutes, before Charlotte's name rose to the surface. She was listed as a Baumann as I had thought. Seeing her name gave me a strange feeling, taking me back to the circumstances of her life and the days and months leading up to her birth.

"Charlotte's grave is deep inside the cemetery," the Director told us, "I will take you to it."

It seemed more and more likely that Emilie and the Prince had waited as long as they did to have a child because they realised the danger any baby they produced would be in. Maybe Emilie begged August to allow her this one thing and he eventually decided to indulge her, knowing how much else she had sacrificed in order to be there waiting for him whenever he returned home from his duties with the army. This was purely guesswork because there were some questions I knew it was unlikely we would ever be able to find the answers to, no matter how long we hunted. Would the gravestone supply me with any information, or was I going to arrive at the grave only to be disappointed once more? After all these years, would the writing on the stone have been eroded away?

As we began our long walk to find Charlotte's final resting place, I peered at the many headstones we passed, and any hopes that I harboured quickly faded when I saw that many of the inscriptions were no longer legible. Ken was holding my hand as we followed the woman on what seemed like an endless journey to meet Charlotte.

In the days when Charlotte was born, succession was a more precarious business than it is today. Early death could strike at any time when kings and princes were as liable as any other soldier to die in battle or of incurable diseases. As we had discovered, they could even be murdered by members of their own family. Thrones were always in danger of being usurped by new family members who felt they had a valid claim. I could understand now that a pregnant Emilie would have been seen as a terrible potential threat by the King and his advisors. Once the baby was born to the couple, she too would be in tremendous danger. The fact that Charlotte was allowed to survive and went on to live to the age of 68, finally dying in 1906, was something of a miracle when you considered the forces stacked against her.

"I hope it won't be long now," the Director said as we walked on and on.

I felt increasingly emotional as we made our way through the rows and rows of headstones in search of this poor woman who had been cut off and rejected by her birth family and forgotten by history. By the time we found her I wasn't able to stop the tears from brimming up. I couldn't believe that we were actually standing in front of Charlotte's grave and that I was reading the inscription. "CHARLOTTE BAUMANN, BORN GOTTSCHALK," and the date was still visible. "SEPTEMBER 25TH, 1838."

"It all fits, Ken," I said. "The false birth name and the date. Charlotte would have been around five years old when her father died in 1843, just as she always said."

After so many years of searching and wondering I had found the final resting place of my great grandmother, Anna's mother and Emilie's lost child, buried next to her husband, Sigmund. How different everything could have been for dear Charlotte.

Ken said nothing, just putting his arm around my shoulders to comfort me as I sobbed partly from sadness at the thought of what she must have gone through as a child, and partly with relief at the fact that I had finally found her. Vandals had split the headstone in two. I couldn't imagine who would have done such a thing as I knelt down and stroked the broken stone.

"Don't worry, Charlotte," I said out loud, "we've found you now. I'll put this right."

It appeared that Charlotte's one lucky break was to have been born a girl. Had she been a boy it seemed unlikely that Wittgenstein and his cronies would have taken the risk of sparing her life once the Prince, her father and protector, was gone. Charlotte herself must have been confused about exactly what had happened between her parents and the rest of the Hohenzollern family, so it was not surprising that her descendants became even more confused as the stories became distorted from inaccurate retelling. But what exactly did she know, and did she pass on all that she knew? Why was her daughter, Anna, so convinced of her own Jewish background? Was she trying to protect Anna from something in the same way that my father Hans had been trying to protect me?

Charlotte had on more than one occasion told her amused grandsons that she really was a duchess, but that didn't mean that Anna, to whom Charlotte gave birth when she was 26 years old, could have ever realised that she was not Jewish. No doubt she heard her mother's stories too, but the everyday evidence that she was a Gottschalk descendant as well as a Baumann must have outweighed what must have sounded very much like childhood fantasies on Charlotte's part. I thought again of my grandmother and how different her final days would have been if fate had dealt the family just a few different cards: if there hadn't been so many secrets and so much confusion and conspiracy. What a long journey it was from the glittering ballroom where August and Emilie met to whatever terrible place their granddaughter, Anna, had died in.

I later discovered something extraordinary had happened concerning the young Charlotte, presumably shortly after she had married her next-door neighbour, Sigmund Baumann. A compelling document had turned up amongst my father's papers. It confirmed that Charlotte's husband had been discharged from the Army. Uncle Freddy's wife, Alice, then revealed to me that my uncle knew Charlotte had written to the King, she would have been just seventeen years old. Charlotte was appealing to the King for her husband's return from Luxembourg and for him to be discharged from the army. That must have been December 1855 as that is the date on his discharge papers. Alice could not tell me why Charlotte had made this request. I could not even speculate why she would do this, but as the document reveals, the king complied. Her ability to achieve that suggested that even at that stage there was still some acceptance within the royal household of the connection between the families. Despite everything that had happened, however, it seems that the family did not completely cut Charlotte off and she must have known more about her past than she divulged to her grandchildren.

Although I now knew for sure that Charlotte had been born to August and Emilie while they were married, and I knew where she had ended up, I still had no idea what had happened to her during the years immediately after her father died. What had led to her becoming a Gottschalk rather than a Hohenzollern like her father, or a von Ostrowska like her mother? I now knew that August had a personal connection to the Gottschalks through Isadore, his tailor, and through Isadore's daughter and the scandal that had erupted as a result of her allegations of seduction levelled against him, but that still didn't explain what had happened regarding Charlotte. Would I ever discover the truth?

CHAPTER
TWENTY-FIVE

The Final Piece of the Puzzle

Even after finding her grave I never gave up my searching or my wondering about her early years, in fact in many ways it increased my feelings of having a personal obligation to her to uncover the hidden truth. I felt certain that the answers must be lying somewhere, if I could just find out where. Perseverance had paid off so many times over the years that I couldn't give up now, that wasn't an option.

I wasn't alone in my preoccupations as I had Dr Henning in Berlin. His wife, Herzeleide, who was head librarian at the archive in Dahlem, was just as keen to help us. In fact she and her husband both became close friends during those later years, taking the quest as personally as I did. Herzeleide would pick up information like postcards, graphics, anything that crossed her path and send it to me in England. On our many trips to Berlin, Ken and I would go to their apartment for dinner and talk endlessly about our mutual passion.

By now, many years after our memorable week of research together in the East German archives, Herr Waltmann had risen to become Director. The Foreign Office's intervention had saved the situation and our relationship had continued uninterrupted. Herr Waltmann was certainly not a man to bear grudges, and I have absolutely no doubt that he had nothing to do with the espionage approach made to Ken. On several occasions, more than ten years after we had first visited him, he sent me further documents, as he did on the day when he found a copy of August's will and sent us a copy. It was an extraordinary discovery, full of detail which made for fascinating reading, knowing as we did by then most of the people named in it. This was the final piece of the puzzle.

Emilie, we could now see, had been provided with a substantial pension for life (1500 taler a year, which was the same allowance she had been receiving while her husband was alive). She had also been left a Mila old master portrait of herself, painted in 1838 at a time when the King was on record as having commissioned separate portraits of the whole family, and a miniature, both in gilded frames. August was probably the one who included her amongst the family sitters, quite possibly without the King's knowledge. The miniature was probably produced from that same sitting as was the custom. That was the picture which we still had in the family. It had been assessed by experts who had been sure that the head had been painted by a master and the body by a student. Paul Mila used to work a lot for the royal family.

223

August's will further stipulated that Emilie was also allowed to keep the silver that was already at her apartment on Jaegerstrasse where she had lived much of the time when he was away — a silver presentation tray and four plain silver candlesticks were also listed. There was no mention in the will of Agnes Gottschalk.

At the same time as trying to track down what had happened to Charlotte, I also wanted to trace any living descendants of August and his first two wives. With the help of the great genealogist Arthur Addington, I eventually managed to trace the family of Eduard von Waldenburg, the son of August's first wife, Friederike von Waldenburg.

When I made contact I discovered that just a few weeks before I got there Eduard's grandson, Siegfried, had died; another link with the past severed forever. His widow, Jutta (who had been born as Princess von Alten), however, agreed to meet us. She was a well-built, Germanic-looking woman with jet-black hair and I could see when we first walked through the door of her apartment that she was wary and suspicious of what our motives might be for seeking her out and seemed reluctant to give anything away. Despite whatever reservations she might have been harbouring, however, she sat us down graciously amidst the many books, pictures and ornaments she had inherited from her own and her husband's families, and calmly listened to our story. As I talked I passed the pocket-book over to her and I saw that I had immediately caught her attention as she turned it over in her hands, stroking the silver gilt cover before opening it up and reading the inscription inside.

"*Mein Gott!*" she exclaimed and from that moment she opened up, her story flowing forth like a river. What she told us explained completely why she had been so guarded when we first arrived. She admitted that her late husband, Siegfried, had been one of Hitler's most admired generals. I was shocked. Our story had started with the battles against Napoleon and now we were hearing about how Hitler had also played a part in our family history, the man who would ultimately be responsible for driving us out of Germany and almost certainly for Anna's death. The family's path became more perverse with every new twist we uncovered.

Apparently now relaxing in our company, Jutta brought out a secret stack of photographs and proudly laid them out in front of us, pointing out the ones that showed her husband standing beside the Führer in full uniform, like the trusted aide he must have been. It was unsettling to be looking at pictures of a man who had brought so much fear and horror to our own childhoods, and had caused so much death and destruction within our families, and to be talking to someone whose husband had been part of Hitler's inner circle but who had also shared a great-grandfather with Anna, a woman who was almost certainly one of the millions murdered on the orders of the dictator in the picture. As Jutta talked I couldn't help remembering the night we listened as a family to Hitler coming to power, the day I proudly and innocently raised the Nazi flag and marched at the head of my class, and the sight of my grandmother's figure disappearing from my eyes for the last time in the steam on the railway platform in Prague.

Jutta went on to tell us how her son-in-law, a captain in the army called von Wallenberg, had been one of the conspirators involved in the plot to assassinate Hitler with a bomb. I clearly remembered hearing of the incident in London. When the bomb first went off it was announced on the radio that Hitler had been killed. As soon as they discovered that he had survived, Jutta's daughter and son-in-law tried to escape from Germany in disguise, but failed. When von Wallenberg was caught he was executed and strung up on a meat hook.

"Nobody around here knows who I am," Jutta admitted in a whisper, as if she still feared being overheard, even in the privacy of her own apartment. "I tell nothing to anyone, but you are different. I will tell you something I have never told anyone. This pocket-book would definitely have belonged to Prince August. It would have been part of a set of his visitors' books that Siegfried inherited. I recognise it. It is the same design. We buried the whole collection in the woods on our estate in East Prussia when the Russians stormed in at the end of the war. We were fleeing for our lives and only just managed to escape, so we couldn't take many possessions with us. And of course we were never able to go back for them because after the war they were on the other side of the wall."

We had brought a photograph of the diary with us. "I will gladly sign it," she said, and duly did so, confirming its provenance.

"You know," she said, "August married Friederike morganatically. In Germany at that time it was just a civil ceremony where the ring was placed on the bride's other hand."

That confirmed yet again what we had already discovered about the financial and inheritance agreements within the Hohenzollern family. I felt we were finally beginning to understand the full complexity and danger of the world that poor little Emilie von Ostrowska entered the night that she allowed Prince August to bewitch her at the ball in his palace. Jutta showed us a ribbon that she used to wear to functions, which had a medallion on it bearing a picture of August. It seemed strange to be shown by someone else a picture of a man I had now grown used to thinking of as being my great, great grandfather. By the time we left Jutta's home we had become firm friends and had promised to stay in touch with anything new we might discover.

Despite the inevitable dead-ends that we were continuing to come up against, we had made substantial progress overall. Encouraged by my successes, I delved further to try to find out if there were any descendants of August's second wife, Auguste, still alive, but all my enquiries led nowhere. After several generations it was beginning to look as if that strand of August's family had ended. Then out of the blue, I received a letter from a Mrs Ritchie, a lady who lived north of London and had heard about my story. Mrs Ritchie turned out to be a revelation. She was the great, great granddaughter of Prince August and

Auguste von Prillwitz. Ken and I gladly accepted a generous lunch invitation to her home.

When we arrived there we were met at the door by a charming lady who greeted me with the words, "Hello cousin." She took us on a guided tour of the house, introducing me to August's paintings which she had inherited from her mother. The dining room had been laid up for lunch with the most beautiful silver, which Mrs Ritchie told us the Prince had once possessed, part of the same collection that Emilie inherited when her husband died. It gave a tiny, modest hint of the splendour our great, great grandparents must once have lived in.

Mrs Ritchie confirmed that August and Auguste had been morganatically married as well, and that Auguste had developed cancer and died at around the time the Prince met young Emilie and fell in love once again.

To be eating lunch surrounded by August's possessions and hearing stories about the various members of the Prillwitz family who were depicted in the paintings on the walls was a wonderful experience. After spending so many years staring at dry, written accounts and descriptions, Mrs Ritchie's home brought the past to life before my eyes.

My searches in Berlin also led me to find descendants of the Ostrowskis. I located Egbert von Ostrowski, a lawyer and head of the family. He and his petite wife, Hildegard, lived in Southern Germany. When I wrote to introduce myself to them they immediately invited us to their home. When we got there we found they were a warm and happy couple.

Through sharing our mutual family histories we became close friends.

By that time I had managed to find out a little more from the Dahlem Archive of what had happened to the tragic Emilie after she was widowed and parted from Charlotte. I could not imagine how she could have ever got together with another man, not to mention falling in love again. Despite that, or maybe because of her vulnerable position, I discovered that she married a Swiss count who owned an estate in West Prussia. As Emilie was on a pension, August's estate was informed of her change of circumstances in writing.

Given what had happened to her over the previous few years, it seems likely that she was marrying for security rather than love, but whatever the reason, I learned from another archive that she later returned alone to Berlin, which suggests the marriage was not a success. I can't help wondering whether that might have been because August had been the love of her life and no other man was likely to be able to live up to such a charismatic, powerful and romantic figure. I could certainly understand if that was the case because I had fallen under his spell myself just by reading about him. The records showed that after leaving the Count she returned to her late father's home in Mohrenstrasse, where she lived with her sister Helena once more, just as she had when they were young girls.

As I grew to know Emilie, I understood that money wasn't of all that much importance to her, over and above the need to pay her way. She must have been in a very poor state by then, maybe because by marrying the

Count she had forfeited her right to a royal pension, and perhaps she even lost the will to live. It was heartbreaking for me when I found her death registered in West Berlin in 1865. She was only 48 years old and the entry reported that she had fallen ill and died at a local hospital, where she was taken by an "unknown man". Upon her death she was registered as a "divorced woman". It was such a tragic end for the young girl who had sacrificed everything for the man she loved.

Being separated from her only child must have been a terrible blow for Emilie and I would imagine that many women would find it hard to be happy ever again after an experience like that. Knowing that as an adult Charlotte definitely talked to my father and uncle about her memories of being with her natural parents when she was very small and of playing with her father on the floor of their apartment, there was no end to my frustration when I could still not find any records of her childhood anywhere. If Anna had ever known any more about her mother's early years she certainly didn't confide it to me or to either of her sons. There was nothing to tell me that Charlotte had ever officially existed apart from her gravestone.

Just as I had with August and Charlotte, I felt I had to make a pilgrimage to Emilie's place of rest when I discovered she was buried in the Ostrowski family grave in the Alte Friedhof.

"You're lucky," Dr Henning informed me. "It's the oldest cemetery in Berlin. It will still be there."

But when we got there Ken and I discovered to our horror that the cemetery had been dug up six months before to make way for a motorway flyover. There was nothing left of the Ostrowski family tomb. It felt like a heartbreakingly desolate end to a sad life.

One day a short while later, Ken and I called into the National Galerie while on a visit to Berlin on the off chance that they might have an oil painting of Prince August. I had been desperate to find a picture of him for a long time. I explained my connection to the man at the gallery.

"We have a Franz Kruger portrait right now down in our cellar," he said. "It's just come back from an exhibition."

I felt my heartbeat quicken as he led us through a maze of corridors and staircases. Ten minutes later we were facing my great, great grandfather and I gazed at him in amazement. The handsome hero of our story inspired me, standing there tall and uniformed in front of me, in the Yellow Chamber of his Bellevue Palace. In the background was hanging a portrait of his beloved Juliette Recamier.

Every time I stumbled across a new connection to the Prince it felt like I was seeing an old friend, getting to know him a little bit more with each meeting.

"I have found your Prince August," my friend, Ernest Lunn, announced happily over the phone to me on another occasion.

"What do you mean?" I asked.

"I have found another portrait of him."

It turned out that the Wallace Collection, a museum on Manchester Square in London, were displaying a miniature painting of the Prince by the French artist, Jean-Baptiste Isabey. I immediately went round and introduced myself. I met Mr Larkworthy, who seemed quite captivated by my story and my connection to the miniature. He was very accommodating, saying we could come back to view the miniature in private, and maybe photograph it.

A few days later, armed with a camera, Ken, Anthony and I entered the upstairs room to see August beautifully displayed before us. Without telling me, Mr Larkworthy had removed the back of the little portrait and there exposed before us were five locks of August's hair. It was simply breathtaking. The hair was auburn brown and not black as I had been led to believe. Mr Larkworthy said that in the many years the little portrait had belonged to the museum it had never been opened up. It had certainly been a day to remember.

CHAPTER
TWENTY-SIX

Tracking Down Isadore and Charlotte

The only part of the family left about whom I still knew very little, as I hadn't been able to track down any of the descendants, were the mysterious Gottschalks. In the course of my searching I came across a book called *Jewish Burghers of the City of Berlin* by a man called Jacob Jacobson, which confirmed that Isadore Gottschalk had indeed lost his citizenship because of debts at one stage of his life and had ended up languishing in a debtors' prison. Later in the book Jacobson wrote that Isadore was released and had his citizenship returned without going into any of the sordid and scandalous details on how that was achieved. So many of the pieces of the story were beginning to fit together, but still no one was able to explain to me what had happened to Charlotte after the Prince's death, or how she had become a Gottschalk. I needed that information in order to complete the whole picture.

Whenever I visited relatives I was always asking questions, hoping that I would stumble across some forgotten nugget of information that would lead on to a new strand of investigation. During a conversation with Freddy's widow, Alice, she suddenly came out with the news that she remembered my uncle had told her that Charlotte had grown up in Hamburg. This came as a revelation. No one had ever mentioned it before. I wondered if there was any chance that she might have left a trace of herself somewhere in some archive records there. I had discovered that in those days travellers entering that city, which was situated in an entirely separate State, would have been required to sign an entry book on arrival at the border control. I wondered if we would be able to find any sign of the Gottschalk family's arrival there from Berlin. I somehow managed to persuade Ken to travel with me to Hamburg even though he was completely convinced that we wouldn't find anything.

At the Hamburg Archive we requested copies of the entry books for the years after August's death and very soon the archivist came back with all the relevant books.

"We're looking at the years around 1845," Ken explained, "although it's pure guesswork."

We thought that if Charlotte was moving to Hamburg it could be a year or two after her father's death. The archivist searched for a while and then found Isadore's signature, pointing it out to us.

"It says he arrived 'with family'," I said excitedly.

"Yes, that would mean he had a child with him," the man confirmed.

234

Although there were no details of the child's name, it seemed very likely it was Charlotte. All the facts fitted in with her story. She would have been about seven, and maybe Isadore was taking her to be raised by Friederike, who we had discovered from another source had moved to Hamburg with her husband after Agnes was born. Isadore himself would have been elderly by then, and there was no mention in any of the archives of his wife still being alive, so bringing up a child would probably have been a daunting prospect for him.

This trip to Hamburg would have meant Charlotte was breaking her last remaining link to Emilie. She would have had only the pocket-book to remind her of who her father and mother were and what they had meant to one another. She had written notes in the book about what might well have been her last meeting with Emilie, when she said "*my beloved mother gave me a beautiful dress for Whitsun*", and then very tellingly in her own childish scrawl, "*this book once belonged to my beloved mother*". There were no further mentions of any meetings with Emilie.

"You are very lucky that they had saved all these records," the archivist said. "Many archives were destroyed in the war, and very little has survived."

It was a huge step forward. I had caught a glimpse of young Charlotte Gottschalk for the first time in her life, but that still didn't tell me how and why she became a Gottschalk in the first place.

When we got back to England I could see that Ken was exhausted. He believed that after all the years we had been searching we had now found all we were ever likely to find.

"It's enough," he would tell me when I would start going over the same ground yet again, trying to see if there was some obvious clue that I was missing. I simply had to get to the bottom of this and was aware that it had become something of an obsession for me. On most days I would be talking to contacts in England and in Germany on the phone or writing them letters, going over and over the same facts like a dog with an old bone just in case it still has a shred of meat clinging to it somewhere.

"Evi," he said one evening when he found me asleep over a table of papers, "it's time to let go. It's time to face facts. There's nothing there. The King destroyed all the evidence. Do you think he wanted future generations to find proof of Charlotte's existence? You have done incredibly well to find as much as you have."

"I need to know, Ken," I protested, shaking myself awake. "I can't get it out of my mind."

"Evi, we have the family to think of, and we can't have a normal conversation any more. You're working at this all the time, day and night. Isn't it about time you gave yourself a rest and started living with your family again? The ones who are actually alive?"

"We've only got a little more to do," I said, realising that he was right but not being able to face the prospect of giving up now, after so many years of searching. "We've got to keep going, Ken. I'm sure the end is in sight."

For the eternally patient and understanding Ken to have finally spoken out so vehemently suggested to me that maybe I had allowed the whole hunt for the truth to take over my life to an unhealthy degree. But there was still that one missing piece in my jigsaw and if I could just find that I was confident the whole picture would finally come into focus. I was going to have to face it, I had become an ancestry-addict, always thinking I would be able to give up my habit after one more fix, but never quite able to.

The questions that were tantalising me now were all connected to how Charlotte had disappeared and suddenly, on her own admission, appeared to start a completely new life at the age of five. How did August and Emilie hide and protect Charlotte from their enemies? Where was she officially registered as a Gottschalk? Where was her birth registered?

For inspiration I re-read Emilie's pleading letter to the King, written soon after August died and just before her whole world fell apart. A real and vibrant connection had formed between Emilie and me, a friendship and an understanding. Poor Emilie, without August and her father, who could she turn to? She must have been in a desperate situation. I was asking her to give me answers about so many things, I needed her to help me solve the puzzle. Emilie was a woman of integrity and apparently a good mother; surely, I thought, she would have wanted to baptise her first-born child, but would that baptism have been recorded, and where?

I realised that Ken was right and I made a big effort to ensure that I didn't neglect him or my sons in the following months, but I can't say that I ever stopped thinking about this one last puzzle because I didn't. I had started my searches in Merseburg in 1973 and nearly fourteen years later I was still racking my brain, trying to imagine what those last days together must have been like. It was a quiet moment one evening, when Ken was happily reading his book, that I was imagining myself right there in the Berlin flat with Emilie and Charlotte. August was still alive and they were still a family unit. I allowed my mind to roam around the imaginary room, becoming completely lost in my thoughts. Out of the corner of my eye I spotted a statue of the Madonna on the imaginary sideboard.

"Of course," I shouted, making Ken jump and snap his book shut, losing his place. "That's it."

"What now?" he asked testily.

"It's been staring at me all the time."

"What has?"

"Charlotte wasn't Jewish."

"Yes, yes, we all know that, Evi."

"No, don't you see?" I ignored his irritability, too excited to be able to contain my own excitement. "We've been looking in the wrong places. We've been looking in the Jewish archives. Emilie would have baptised her baby, I'm sure of that. She was from a Polish Christian family. So there's only one place Charlotte can be. We need to go back."

"Not back to the East," he said and I could see he was adamant.

"No, not the East," I said quickly, wanting to reassure him. "Just to Berlin. I need to go back there, Ken. Just one more time. The answer's there, I can feel it."

I knew that I was stretching his patience to breaking point, but I also knew that he would ultimately do anything for me when he understood it meant so much. I knew that because he had proved it so often before. I was right and a few days later we were back on the plane to Berlin for our umpteenth visit since the hunt began. When we landed we went straight to the Church Registry archive, hoping against hope that August and Emilie would have registered Charlotte's baptism. The archivist understood exactly what I was looking for and left us to see whether she could locate the relevant information. She returned within no more than five minutes.

"Another dead end, Ken," I sighed as I saw her approaching. We were about to thank the lady and say our goodbyes when she said, "Here it is, Mrs Haas."

"I'm sorry," I replied. "Here is what?"

"The entry you are looking for."

No, impossible. The archivist handed the book to us. It couldn't be. I covered my face with my hands, peering through my fingers, terrified that at any moment I was going to wake up and discover the whole thing was a dream. The year was 1838. I read it out loud to Ken, my voice quivering with the effort of holding back some tears.

"August Gottschalk, a shoemaker's apprentice registers his wife, Dorothee Granzow, a Polish woman, and the birth of their daughter Charlotte Dorothee Souife Gottschalk."

"We've found them. We've done it. They hid her from danger and at the same time legitimised her."

It was all over. We had reached our destination. The archivist stood there, bemused as I poured congratulations and gratitude over her. Ken knew exactly how much this discovery would mean to me. We were both ecstatic. This simple little entry would have thrown up a dozen different questions if we had come across it at the beginning of our search, before we had managed to find so many other details about both the Hohenzollern and the Gottschalk families. But because of our researches we already knew that Sophia Dorothea was the name of August's grandmother — she was also the daughter of England's King George I — so registering their daughter as Dorothee Souife (the German equivalent) and Emilie taking Granzow as her own name clearly referred both to the Hohenzollern connections and her Polish descent. So I was certain that this was Emilie disguising herself but leaving just enough clues for me to find her.

August's princely pride hadn't quite allowed him to hide his identity completely either, even at the moment of perpetrating this deception. While he had been willing to pretend to take on the name of Gottschalk to save his daughter's life, he had still retained his own first name at the last moment. It was typical of August to register a Jewish family name in a church archive, thumbing his nose at the anti-Semitic establishment. At the time of the registration Emilie and baby Charlotte would have been back in Berlin, ensconced in the flat that August had arranged for them in Jaegerstrasse.

The Berlin Registry entry stated that the child was registered on 28 October when the couple came back from Prillwitz, and Emilie had got over the birth. The date on Charlotte's gravestone must have been a guess, much as the date on the marriage certificate had been, as Charlotte would not have known her real birth date without access to any of the legitimate records or papers, which would have told her the truth. Everything about Charlotte's existence — when, where and how she had arrived on this earth — had been based on falsified information.

Suddenly I had to get used to this whole new situation. As I chattered excitedly away with Ken I could tell that he had truly believed there was nothing more to find out. In one sense he may have been right but somehow I still felt that we had not reached the end of our quest along the trail that led from August and Emilie, through Charlotte to her daughter, my grandmother Anna, of whose fate I still knew very little. Therefore my journey would not be over until I had truly discovered the ending of her story.

CHAPTER
TWENTY-SEVEN

The Vanished Palace

I could now begin to picture much more clearly what must have happened at the start of Charlotte's life. When they first found out that Emilie was pregnant the King and Wittgenstein must have been furious, knowing that the rules of the morganatic marriage would have less power over the rights of a hereditary aristocrat like Emilie than they had had over Friederike and Auguste, the Prince's first two wives, both of whom were only bestowed with titles by the King. Even though she was so young and innocent, only 21 years old at the time of the conception, a pregnant Emilie posed a greater danger to the massive royal fortunes that had come to lie in her husband's hands than either of her predecessors, and so did her unborn child, particularly if it had turned out to be a boy.

For all we knew, of course, there may have been many other failed attempts on her life that were never documented. Poor Emilie was lucky indeed to have been allowed to live long enough to have her child. The fates, it seemed, were willing our family to survive.

When the child was born and found to be a girl, the couple's enemies may well have relaxed a little since it was not usual for a woman to get hold of a European throne, however strong her claim (although of course her male heirs could have claims). However such things did happen and Queen Victoria, a distant relative of both August and the King, had ascended the British throne only the year before, so however small the chances, they would still have been wary of the potential threat this baby girl posed.

August already knew about the very real attempts on Emilie's life and now he had a child to protect from his political enemies as well. He knew better than anyone that there were plenty of people who would have wanted Charlotte to disappear or meet with a tragic accident, and that there was plenty of money available to pay for such dark deeds to be perpetrated without the trail of guilt leading back to the King or to Wittgenstein. His family history was littered with similar ruthless acts when thrones and great fortunes were at stake. The Prince must therefore have decided right from the start that Charlotte needed to be given a different identity, even though he and Emilie intended to keep her with them and bring her up themselves. It was like preparing a hiding place for her to go to should she need it. To provide that false identity he turned to the Jewish community, a people he had shown great loyalty to, particularly through his championing of Major Meno Burg.

He must have reasoned that a Jewish family would be guaranteed to be outside the political intrigues of the royal circle, particularly a humble family like the Gottschalks with whom he already had a connection because of Isadore's services to his family as a tailor and because of his alleged fathering of Isadore's grandchild, Agnes. If Charlotte was to take on their name legally the chances of her ever being a threat to the royal family in those anti-Semitic times was almost guaranteed to disappear.

At some stage August must have gone to see Isadore, with whom he must have patched up his previous difficulties, and suggested they concoct a plan together. August already knew enough about Isadore to make a judgement as to whether or not he could trust him with this precious secret. He must have decided that he could. The Gottschalk family were also dependent on him for the continued support of Agnes as well as on his patronage of Isadore's tailoring services, so it would have been in their interests to do as he asked of them.

Her father's relatively premature death left little Charlotte in a state of limbo. She was legally registered as a Gottschalk even though she had quite possibly never met the family personally, having been living with her biological mother and father despite her unusual legal status.

If Wittgenstein knew about the whole plan, which he almost certainly did even if August hadn't informed him personally, given that information was what he was best at collecting, he would have taken advantage of the situation. He probably insisted and convinced the King that now August was gone and Charlotte no longer had his protection, Emilie must give her up and that

Charlotte must go to live full-time with the family she was registered as belonging to. Wittgenstein would have reasoned that once she was accepted as being a Gottschalk she would no longer be any threat to the King at all and all the issues and claims would be put to rest forever.

No doubt there was some money in the arrangement for Isadore Gottschalk to help him pay for the upkeep of the child, but it is also likely he was given no choice in the matter. A Jewish family living in anti-Semitic Prussia at that time would not have been in a position to argue with a powerful figure like Prince Wittgenstein. They might even have seen it as an advantage to have a royal baby in the family.

I can only hope that the Gottschalks were kind to the little girl who was foisted on them by people who were in many ways their worst enemies. It must have been an appalling trauma for a little girl to lose her father and grandfather and then almost immediately to be removed from her mother and from her home and housed with complete strangers. She told her grandsons, my father and his brother, that she was a "duchess" when in reality she was a virtual orphan. Since she left no written memories beyond the pages that I had studied in such detail in the pocket-book, I have to accept that we will never know any more of the domestic details of how she fared in those early years of her life as a Gottschalk. Anything she eventually told the family apparently came out hesitatingly and cloaked in mystery, so the real story that Charlotte had to tell died with her. When Charlotte played games with her father the Prince she would never have known that her real identity had already been hidden for her own protection, she was far too young. If she knew enough as an adult to write to the King on her husband's behalf, she must have found out later.

As he had written in the diary, August was Emilie's "protector". With him gone Emilie was virtually helpless to protect her little daughter or herself. She would have known from her own experiences that the threat of assassination was very real and she must have felt she was being torn in two. Having lost her beloved husband, her father and her friend, Uhde, she must have wanted to cling to her daughter like never before. At the same time she would have seen the grave danger to both her and the child if she had tried to fight the Establishment and keep hold of Charlotte after receiving Wittgenstein's curt letter. Whatever the truth of the events that followed, Charlotte had undoubtedly been forced out of her mother's hands. How lonely the future must have looked to Emilie at the moment when she lost her royal child to another family, where she would disappear from sight.

Finally the entire picture was almost in focus. With the help of the letter from Emilie to the King, the falsely registered birth at the Church Registry, the entry book in Hamburg and the gravestone inscription, I could now trace where Charlotte had been in those early years and I was now nearly ready to leave these people whom I had spent so many years tracking down and getting to know. Even I could see that there was probably nothing more that I would be able to learn of

Emilie and Charlotte. It felt like it was time to leave them to rest in peace, and to do that I wanted to return to the place where the whole story started.

I wanted to find Wilhelmstrasse 65, the palace where August and Emilie met for the first time at the grand ball and instantly fell in love, setting in motion the whole story that would eventually lead to my life and the lives of my three sons. I expected to find that it had been turned into an office block or a hotel, or possibly a shopping arcade, but I hoped I would still be able to see at least some of its former glory.

But when I got to Wilhelmstrasse the palace wasn't there. Where it should have been there was just an empty gap in the buildings like an ugly missing tooth. Greatly disappointed to have been cheated of a glimpse of the magnificent building I had read so much about in the archives, my curiosity was piqued once more. What was it that had finally wiped it away? Had it been bombed during the war? What had happened to it? I went to look through the local records and found that August's sister, Luise, and her husband, Prince Anton Radziwill, sold the palace to the King and the state after August's death. What they could never have anticipated when they made that decision was the gruesome fate that lay in store for the beautiful building.

Over the following century the anti-Semitism of powerful people such as Wittgenstein grew darker and deeper, taking a firm hold on the hearts and minds of an increasingly angry and embittered people, eventually culminating in the rise of the Nazi Party and the events that led to the deaths of so many millions of Jews from families just like ours. When Adolf Hitler seized power he requisitioned the palace at Wilhelmstrasse 65 and made it part of his infamous Chancellery complex. He occupied August's palace and made it his feared Ministry of Justice. The terrible truth gradually dawned on me as I studied the pictures in the local archives. It was in the very ballroom that August and Emilie met for the first time that Hitler ratified the Final Solution, delivering a signature that led directly to the death of their granddaughter, Anna, my grandmother, as Hitler invaded Czechoslovakia 110 years after the lovers' first dance together.

Hitler was a fanatical admirer of Frederick the Great and if he had known the full story of Anna's ancestry, and that she was the King's great niece, surely he would never have sanctioned what happened to her? He almost certainly knew that Jutta's husband, one of his trusted generals, was a descendant of Prince August and admired him for it, but about Anna and her line he would have known nothing. She, like the rest of our family, was just part of a troublesome statistic in need of a solution.

The building, which had grown to be one of the most infamous in European history, had been symbolically destroyed by the Russians when they marched into Berlin at the end of the Second World War.

I believed that I understood what had driven Emilie to make the decisions she did on the day she fell in love with the Prince. But when she received the letter from Wittgenstein the decision was made for her. Her beloved child was wrenched from her grasp and lost to the Gottschalks. Emilie was not a person ever to be motivated by the pursuit of power and wealth. I truly think that at that ball in Wilhelmstrasse, when she was still little more than a child, she fell deeply in love with one of the most charismatic men in the world at the time, and he with her. I believe it was love that kept them together against the odds for the next eleven years and led to them defying the King and creating a child of their own.

I understand what it feels like to be in love like that because I too fell in love with one man and stayed happily married to him for 42 years until he died in 1990.

Emilie must have known from the beginning that if she agreed to a relationship with August she would be shunned by the Royal Court, even though she probably didn't fully understand the implications at her age. And she would very quickly have been warned that a baby would have been most unwelcome in the Royal Establishment, but she went ahead with it anyway. It had been a truly great romance.

Shortly before he died Ken told me he had enjoyed every moment of the hunt for August, Emilie and Charlotte, and that the years we spent working together on the search were the happiest of his life.

CHAPTER
TWENTY-EIGHT

A Letter from the Grave

As I grew older I found my thoughts returning more and more often to the final days and years of the life of my grandmother Anna. Never a day went by when I didn't think fondly of her. It was only after both my mother and my Uncle Freddy had been dead for more than ten and fifteen years respectively, that Freddy's widow, Alice, told me in the early 1980s about something that had happened in London a few months after my father's death in 1956.

"One day your mother's doorbell rang," she said. "When she answered it she found an elderly Czech woman standing on the doorstep, clutching a letter. 'I am looking for Hans Jaretzki,' the woman said. 'My name is Edelstein and I knew his mother, Anna. She wrote me a letter in 1942 which I thought her family should have.'"

Puzzled and intrigued, apparently my mother invited the woman in and took the letter from her, explaining that my father had died in March. She recognised her mother-in-law's elegant writing immediately. As she told me the story Alice gave me the letter and as I sat reading it a hundred different emotions bubbled up from inside my heart, threatening to stifle me.

Prague on a Saturday [Anna wrote]. *Most honoured and kind Mrs Edelstein, I am writing these lines in anguish to express my eternal thank you for what you, honoured lady and you sir have done for me. Tomorrow or Monday I will be taken to Theresienstadt. I cry and I cry bitterly. My heart is so weak that I can hardly walk. Hopefully this will not last much longer. I send my warmest greetings to your dear husband, and to you worthy Mrs. E my embrace in spirit.*

Your most esteeming and happy, sad
Frau Jaretzki

It had taken fourteen years for news of Anna's final days to reach the family, and three months longer than my father had been able to wait. If she was taken away in the summer of 1942, that would have coincided with the time that her letters and postcards stopped arriving. Maybe it was a mercy that my father never had to hear the details of what happened to his mother, that he was still able to cling to the faint hope that she might have been allowed to die in her own apartment with dignity and without suffering. Realising that her visitor was entirely genuine in her mission, my mother started to ask her questions and the answers must have rekindled all the fears and horrors that my mother remembered herself from that period, from living in a land where the authorities could do as they wished with you, including putting you to death on no more than a whim.

Alice said that Mrs Edelstein told my mother that the fateful day when Anna was "collected" by the soldiers was 16 July 1942, two days short of the anniversary of her grandfather August's death, 99 years before. The words in her letter showed that she had known her days were numbered even before the SS came knocking on her door at the appointed time and bundled her down the stairs from the top floor flat to the waiting truck outside.

"I learned later," Mrs Edelstein continued, "that the lorry was driven to the outskirts of Prague, from where your mother-in-law and the other passengers were route marched nearly 30 kilometres in the summer heat to their destination, Theresienstadt."

Theresienstadt was a holding station that many thousands of Jews were taken to before they were sent on to Auschwitz and almost certain death. There they were stripped of their possessions and made to sign away any property they might own. In time it became a scene of mass death like the other camps. My father had always hoped against hope that if his mother had been taken, she would have ended her days there in Theresienstadt and not been transported to Auschwitz, but Mrs Edelstein did not know what had happened after Anna walked through those gates. She could not tell my mother whether Anna had made her final journey to the most infamous and horrifying death camp of all.

"As my husband Hans is no longer here," my mother said when her visitor had finished telling her story, "please could you take this letter on to his brother, Freddy."

Mrs Edelstein agreed to take the letter to Uncle Freddy personally. Perhaps she felt she wanted to complete the mission herself after safeguarding the letter for so many years. I can only imagine how Uncle Freddy felt when reading it because he and my mother must have made a pact at that time not to tell anyone else about the letter. It would become yet another secret in a family already burdened with too many, until the day when Alice finally told me of its existence.

As I took in the story that Alice was telling me I was shocked to be confronted with the image of my old granny I remembered and loved so much waiting to be taken away by the Nazis. But at the same time I wanted to know more about what happened to her after she wrote the letter, what her final days had been like, even though I suspected that whatever I found out would break my heart.

I still had my childhood autograph book with her little message to me:

When once you are a grandmamma, and sit in the rocking chair with Grandpapa and dream of your joyful childhood days, remember your Oma Annchen.

I wrote several times to the Czech authorities to try to find out the official version of what had happened to her and in 1984 finally received a reply, nearly thirty years after my father had died not knowing what had happened to his mother and whether she had ended her days in Auschwitz. The communist authority informed me that Anna was collected and taken to Theresienstadt on 16 July 1942 (five days after she had written the letter) and then, only a few weeks later, on 12 August she died there, apparently from typhus. They even provided me with the number of the transport she had been taken on and the plot number that they said was her grave. It seemed her murder was a small cog in a giant and efficiently run machine. I now knew the ghastly truth about my granny's end.

The moment I heard the truth my thoughts went straight to my father and the many years that he had to endure not knowing whether or not his mother had ended her days in Auschwitz. Even though in our darkest moments we had all imagined Anna having to endure even worse suffering than the scenes that Mrs Edelstein had described and the Czech authorities had confirmed, it was hard to have the facts finally made real, to have all hope that Anna had died a dignified and comfortable death removed forever.

Soon after Alice told me about the letter one of my best friends, Hannah Miller, contacted her cousin who lived in Prague and told her the story. Armed with Anna's address in the Praha 6 district, this cousin went off to visit the house, hardly expecting to meet any of the original family who lived there during Anna's final days but hoping to find someone who might remember her. Hannah was an actress and broadcaster for the

BBC World Service, living near Temple Fortune in North London. I would often go to her house and we would read German books out loud together and discuss my progress with my researches. When Hannah had suggested contacting her cousin I had accepted the offer gratefully. Now we waited for her to report back, which she did just a few days later.

"I called at the block and rang the bell at street level," she told us. "A lady in her mid fifties came down to open the door and incredibly then introduced herself as one of the 'Barakova sisters', the daughters of the doctor whose flat it had been when Anna moved in. Both sisters remained unmarried, still living in the same block they had been brought up in as children. She then proceeded to give a vivid account of that fateful July day. 'I remember Anna Jaretzki well,' she said. 'I remember seeing her being collected by the SS and put on a truck, it was a terrible day. That was the last time we saw her. She had to leave everything behind, only allowed to pack one small bag with her things.' "

So many people during those years, including children like these two girls, had been forced to watch so many horrifying things and had been powerless to do anything to stop them, leaving them with images that would doubtless haunt those children for the rest of their lives. The soldiers had ignored the fact that Anna could hardly walk because of the pain in her tired old joints.

"Some young Jews who had already been loaded into the back of the lorry jumped out to help her up when they saw her struggling," Hannah's cousin told us, "only to be mocked by the soldiers for their efforts."

To imagine my poor grandmother Anna struggling to get onto that lorry, trying her hardest to do as she was ordered, is still painful for me, even today.

Having the scene painted so clearly for me at last made it all the more poignant knowing what had happened in Anna's family one hundred years before and how it had come about that she should have ended her days in such a tragic way. The modest, gentle granddaughter of one of the greatest princes in all Europe had ended up dying anonymously in a crowded prison camp because her grandparents had been trying to protect her mother from danger by hiding her identity.

EPILOGUE

Visiting Anna

As I came closer myself to the age she was when I knew her, I felt a growing need to say goodbye to my granny properly, to let her know that her little granddaughter still remembered her and still loved her with all her heart. At the same time I wanted to see if I could come to at least some understanding of how human beings could be so cruel to one another. How could anyone bully to death a defenceless old lady, riddled with arthritis, a woman who had only ever given love to everyone around her? Anna had never made an enemy in the whole of her life, yet these people decided she was their enemy and that she should be robbed and trampled on.

After the Berlin Wall fell in 1989, my son Timothy suggested that he, Ken and I should all travel to Theresienstadt, which was now called Terezin (Ghetto Town). He knew how much I wanted to visit Anna after all the letters she wrote to me expressing her hope that she would see me again. In my mind I was now preparing myself for the possibility that I could make this trip. While I was still getting used to the idea Ken fell ill, and after a lifetime together we were parted when he died on 12 October 1990.

They were of course difficult days for me. I found myself talking to Timothy a great deal about my life and about the stories triggered by the little pocket-book. Just like we did when Ken was around, Timothy and I often used to walk together in Kenwood, the magnificent park close to our home, straddling Hampstead and Highgate. There, still trying to make sense of it all I found myself wondering how much Anna knew about her mother and her grandparents. Had Charlotte confided things to her that she had decided to keep to herself? Believing that Ken had heard all he wanted on the subject, I had bottled up so much over the years, and it all poured out once more as soon as I realised that Timothy, who had been engrossed with his family's past since a young boy, now also felt the urge to visit Terezin to pay his respects to Anna. He was as devoted to the story as I had been, and his support was such a great encouragement to me. Just like Ken he would make me feel safe.

Once I had set my mind on going to Theresienstadt I found that it became a new compulsion, something I felt I had to do. I wanted to "meet" my beloved Annchen again. Other members of the family didn't feel that they could face the emotional pain of such a trip, but Timothy had come to feel exactly as I did about our family history. When he was at boarding school in the years after the war his life had been hard because of his German family background, and he had

countered that by making Germany, Prussia and
Europe, and people who made a difference, a main core
of his film career, which gave him an ability to
understand what life would have been like for August
and Emilie.

It took a little while to arrange everything, but
finally the trip was organised for 2005, more than
thirty years after I first started out on my adventure
through the pocket-book and into the past. Timothy
and I travelled first to Anna's last home in Prague. It
was the first time I had been back to Prague since that
moment when I hugged my grandmother for the very
last time. The area where my uncle had found the
apartment for her was quiet when our hotel driver
drew up, the surrounding parkland eerily inviting. As I
stood by the entrance to the apartment block I could
imagine how frightening the bustle and noise of
German military activity on the streets must have
seemed to those living there, none of them knowing
what all the changes might mean to their lives or what
would be happening to them next.

Despite already feeling deeply emotional as I stared
up at the attic window of Anna's apartment, I didn't
cry. I wanted to be at my best for her, to be as brave
and stoic as she had been on that day in 1942. Timothy
and I then went on to the Jewish Quarter in an ancient
part of the city, where we visited the old synagogue and
the thousand-year-old Jewish cemetery. I had once
been told that all those who had perished in the
Holocaust had had their names painted on the walls of
the synagogue. Although I had known the lists would

be there, it was a shock to actually see so many tens of thousands of names stretching from floor to ceiling on every side of the room. We stood there motionless and in a daze, having no idea where to even start looking for Anna. There was no one for us to ask for help, just the silent walls with their terrible columns of the dead and murdered seeming to go on and on forever.

Then, for no apparent reason, Timothy's eye was caught by a single name in one of the corners, as if it were calling out to catch my attention. "Anna Jaretzka, it's here," he called out. "I've found Anna." It seemed like a miracle.

There she was with her dates, "1864–1942."

I could find no words to express my feelings at that moment. I was struck dumb. I felt uplifted and very emotional to be there and to be reconnecting with Anna at last.

The following day it took us half an hour to drive from where the German lorry would have dropped Anna on the outskirts of the city to the place where she died, and all through the journey I could picture her, a fragile old lady being forced to march in the crushing summer heat. It didn't seem like much had changed in the surrounding countryside over the previous half century. Elderly farm vehicles and carts were virtually the only traffic and there were no newly built houses. Just before we reached the dismal ghetto town we came to an ancient fortress, which the German administration had taken over during those years of occupation. It was 12 August, the 63rd anniversary of Anna's death.

We had an appointment with the Director, inside the fortress. Our driver pulled up at the main entrance, on the other side of a moat bridge, where huge wooden gates barred our way. It was a desolate and godforsaken place.

"We have to be grateful," Timothy said softly, trying to find some words that might comfort me, "that her suffering didn't last long, that she died here and wasn't transported to Auschwitz as your father so feared."

There was no one around and we found it impossible to raise anyone from the entry phone on the wall. With nothing to think about except Anna's final days, we waited for about twenty minutes before finally leaving the car and making the rest of our journey on foot. When we were finally ushered in to meet the Director, Dr Jan Munk, a retired university lecturer who was an expert on the history of the period, we found ourselves in a surreal situation, sitting in the former Kommandant's office. We took a deep breath and pushed the enormity of the moment to the back of our minds so that we could fortify ourselves for what we were about to hear.

"Your grandmother would have been in a barracks called Hanover," Dr Munk explained, "one of the ones for the old people. She came in alone with no family to care for her. At the age of 78 she was bound not to have lasted long. Those who had family to help them tended to live longer and they were the ones who ended up being transported to Auschwitz."

Evidence had recently come to light that people like Anna had been asked by the Nazis to sign a contract with the State at the time they were collected, agreeing that in return for looking after them the State would be given all their money, possessions and valuables. According to Dr Munk, Anna would have been told that she was going to a spa, a sort of retirement home. If she was convinced by such empty promises the illusion would only have lasted until the moment she arrived at this terrible place.

"What happened to the Kommandant?" Timothy enquired.

The reply was direct. "They showed him no mercy of course. He had lived in luxury in this fortress with his family until he was captured after the end of the war and tried by a local court. The man was hanged just outside over there in the courtyard."

I wanted to know everything and I asked question after question. It seemed so extraordinary that one harmless old woman would be worth them going to all this trouble. Why would the mighty German military machine have bothered to mark her down and expend valuable time and manpower on picking her up just so that she could die here? What a terrible madness the whole business had been. Although it was an intensely emotional experience I didn't actually feel depressed by being there and learning the truth first hand. If anything I felt energised by having finally got to this place. Individual details, however, could still bring the tears smarting to my eyes, like the fact that the ashes of the dead, many thousands we were told, were tipped into the river causing it to become choked up, days before the Allies arrived and despite specific promises by the Nazis that they would never do such a thing.

Before we came we had asked Dr Munk if it would be possible for them to make up and erect a memorial stone tablet for Anna. The Doctor was a kind man and he had been receptive to the idea after hearing our story and agreed to do this and allow us to place the tablet in the wall of the columbarium, where the Nazis used to store the ashes of some of the prisoners they cremated. Even though Anna had been buried because the crematorium wasn't built until a year after she died, this seemed a fitting place for her to be remembered. The Director escorted us there personally and I unveiled my dedication to my grandmother in a silent ceremony, taking a firm hold of Timothy's hand for support.

We were then driven to visit the burial ground where Anna's body would have been dumped into the communal graves. The town, we were told, was now being returned to the original families who had lived there before the Germans, and then the Russians, arrived. But all we could see were deserted streets and houses. Not many people, it seemed, were choosing to come back to a place like this if they had an alternative. We entered the open burial ground, walking through a scattering of unnamed stones.

We stopped on the way back at the local school and the Director took us inside. There was a plaque, which said that none of the children from the school during those years had survived; they had all been transported to their deaths.

We returned the following day, still not feeling ready to be finally parted from Anna. This time we went to the Hanover Barracks, Anna's home for the last three weeks of her life, a desolate godforsaken building with huge double wooden doors. I now felt fulfilled rather than sad, content that I had done as much as I possibly could.

There had been a Menorah tree growing in the middle of the burial ground, which struck me as particularly beautiful and poignant in such a terrible place. The plaque under the tree told us that after the war it was found growing in the Theresienstadt ghetto, a sapling that had been planted by the same children who had later been taken away to die in Auschwitz. The authorities had moved it to the burial ground and replanted it in order to remind people that wherever there is death there is also life.

What was so strange and ironical perhaps about Anna's fate, was that the way in which her mother Charlotte was hidden away within a Jewish family was almost a mirror opposite of the biblical story from Genesis — of how Moses was hidden in a basket on the banks of the River Nile to protect him from being killed as a Hebrew baby boy, on the orders of the Pharoah — and how he was later discovered by the Pharoah's daughter in the bulrushes, and subsequently brought up as an Egyptian prince to disguise his Jewish identity. In Charlotte's case, the daughter of a powerful prince, and therefore a princess in her own right, the truth of her ancestry was buried to protect her and as a result her own daughter Anna was to die in Nazi Europe in what was a kind of re-enactment of the Egyptian Holocaust. A further irony was that what had really taken place was also the precise opposite of what my parents had always assumed — that August had entered into a relationship with a woman of humble Jewish origins and that that was the reason why it had been kept secret.

But the final and deepest irony remained that according to the secrets of the pocket-book Anna was the direct descendant of one of the wealthiest and most powerful Prussian princes who ever lived, a member of a family that Hitler himself held in the highest possible regard. Despite all that she had still been unable to save herself in the face of the deeply ingrained prejudice, cruelty and hatred that had shamed all Europe during those years. It was almost too painful to contemplate.

My grandmother Anna had died for the love of August and Emilie and I hoped that I had gone some way to repay the love she had lavished on me as a small child. Over the previous 35 years I had learned so much about humanity and about myself. I had made new friends all around the world, including members of my own family who I had not previously known existed.

When I embarked upon my journey I could never have known what the past was going to reveal to me. I thank God that at the end of it all I can say that Ken, my family and every one of those wonderful people who have been part of this amazing experience with me, can also take credit for helping me to achieve my goal. For we have all of us together given Emilie, Charlotte and Anna back their true identities.

May their souls rest in peace.

Acknowledgements

When I embarked on this mysterious journey of discovery I had no idea what to expect, and where it would take me. Without the unfailing support and guidance given to me from so many, I would not have been able to overcome the numerous obstacles and barriers that confronted me along the way. To them all I owe a deep debt of gratitude.

I extend my warm appreciation to Her Majesty The Queen for granting me her permission to research in the Royal Archive at Windsor. To my dearest friend Hanna Miller, who shared my passion and intrigue with such fervour. Laura Petzal, a great ally and friend, who was available day and night to help me with complicated translations. I cannot forget the wisdom and forethought of Ernest Lunn whose suggestions so often turned into golden nuggets. Especially Nancy Hadwen whose belief in me remained undiminished. Herbert Braunsberg, for all his help, especially for his French translations. Diana Daniels, who typed my early efforts with so much interest and efficiency. My close friend Barbera Barclay, always ready to contribute with her knowledge and Eve Sheldon-Williams, whose lively spirit greatly encouraged me. Tony and Trude Frigeri whose love and help have been such an inspiration. Myoldest friend Stephanie Rosenblatt, the sister I never had, her love and loyalty have been a source of great strength to me throughout my life.

My husband Ken and I spent many happy hours in Berlin with Dr Eckart Henning, in charge of The Hohenzollern archive, and his wife Herzeleide, the Head Librarian. They provided us with a fountain of knowledge and shared the excitement of our discoveries. Through my search I found my new family, so dear to me, Egbert von Ostrowski and his wife Hildegard, and a delightful friendship. My grateful thanks to Jutta von Waldenburg for her help and all that she was able to tell me about our Prussian family. To my cousins Thomas and Alex Jarrett, and to their wives Doris and Pat. When I embarked on my journey to find Emilie I could always rely on their unwavering help and support. My daughter-in-laws Michelle and Brigitte who entered my world with such relish and enthusiasm. And to my brother Claude who I hold dear to my heart; he travelled with me always along my journey.

I would also like to express my deep gratitude to the following individuals and institutions and their helpful staff.

Jeffrey Finestone, Burkes Peerage
David Williamson
John Dudley
Sir Roger Fulford

Ian Bowater
Arthur Addington
Steve Jones
W. F. Ashbrook
Alexe von Brockdorff
Malcolm Kafetz
PhDr Jan Munk CSc., Director of The Terezin
  Memorial
Prof. Frank Eyck, Emeritus Professor of History,
  University of Calgary
Debretts Peerage
W. J. Larkworthy, The Wallace Collection, London
Mark Lefanu, The Society of Authors
The Victoria & Albert Museum
The British Museum
The London Library
The British Library
The Goethe Institute, London
The German Historical Institute, London
The National Gallerie, Berlin
Geheimes Staatsarchiv Preussicher Kulturbesitz,
  Dahlem, West Berlin
Herr Waltmann, Deutches Zentralarchiv, Merseberg,
  East Germany
Southampton University

Also available in ISIS Large Print:

The Man Who Mistook his Wife for a Hat

Oliver Sacks

"He reached out his hand, and took hold of his wife's head, tried to lift it off, to put it on . . . His wife looked as if she was used to such things."

In his most extraordinary book, Oliver Sacks recounts the stories of patients lost in the bizarre, apparently inescapable world of neurological disorders. These are case studies of people who have lost their memories and with them the greater part of their pasts; who are no longer able to recognize people or common objects; whose limbs have become alien; who are afflicted and yet are gifted with uncanny artistic or mathematical talents. In Dr Sacks's splendid and sympathetic telling, each tale is a unique and deeply human study of life struggling against incredible adversity.

ISBN 978-0-7531-5699-5 (hb)
ISBN 978-0-7531-5236-2 (pb)

The Gaol

Kelly Grovier

For over 800 years, Newgate was the grimy axle around which British society slowly twisted. This was where such legendary outlaws as Robin Hood and Captain Kidd met their fates, where the rapier-wielding playwrights Ben Johnson and Christopher Marlowe sharpened their quills, and where flamboyant highwaymen like Claude Duval and James Maclaine made legions of women swoon. While London's theatres came and went, the gaol endured as London's unofficial stage. From the Peasants' Revolt to the Great Fire, it was from Newgate that England's greatest dramas unfolded.

By piecing together the lives of forgotten figures, as well as re-examining the prison's links with more famous individuals from Dick Whittington to Charles Dickens, this thrilling history goes in search of a ghostly place, erased by time, which inspired more poems and plays, paintings and novels, than any other structure in British history.

ISBN 978-0-7531-8460-8 (hb)
ISBN 978-0-7531-8461-5 (pb)

Journey to the Edge of the World

Billy Connolly

From the Atlantic to the Pacific via the fabled Northwest Passage; with idiosyncratic humour, Billy Connolly searches for the beauty of ordinariness and bumps into all manner of weird and wonderful people along the way, from the fiddle-playing scarecrow-maker to the septuagenarian pioneer who still lives as her ancestors did. He learns how not to be intimate with bears and how to pan for gold. He herds cattle, attempts the finer complexities of the Inuit language, jams with fellow musicians and kisses a cod.

At this pivotal moment in history when this once isolated wilderness is about to be invaded by hordes of modern-day speculators, the inimitable Billy retraces the steps of romantics and nutters, the broken-hearted, those looking for love or just hoping to get rich. He leads us through this land's incredible past and shares his optimism about its future.

ISBN 978-0-7531-5695-7 (hb)
ISBN 978-0-7531-5696-4 (pb)

While Flocks Last

Charlie Elder

A worrying number of Britain's birds are in population freefall. We have lost well over half of our familiar house sparrows and starlings over the last 25 years, songbirds haven't much to sing about these days and many birds of woodland, wetland and upland are now living on a wing and a prayer. Armed with a field guide and a half-decent pair of binoculars, Charlie Elder travels the length and breadth of the British Isles to spot 40 bird species in serious decline — the UK's Red List. He looks at why their numbers have fallen, what efforts are being made to encourage their recoveries and meets experts and enthusiasts who are working to make a difference. He also examines just why birds matter in the first place and considers the role of the birdwatcher — one species that is certainly not in decline.

ISBN 978-0-7531-5697-1 (hb)
ISBN 978-0-7531-5698-8 (pb)

Madresfield

Jane Mulvagh

Romantic, turreted, ancient, Madresfield Court has been the home of the Lygon family for over 900 years. Beneath the Malvern Hills, it is a lived-in family home in which the heraldic sits next to the domestic. The Lygons were the inspiration and model for the doomed Marchmain family in Evelyn Waugh's *Brideshead Revisited*: Waugh was a regular visitor in the 1930s, one in a long line of writers, composers, painters, royals and rebels who passed through Madresfield's doors.

Drawing on a unique and virtually unknown archive that dates back to the Conquest, Jane Mulvagh illuminates a rich and dramatic history. From the Lygon who conspired to overthrow Queen Mary in the Dudley plot to the scandal of William Lygon, the disgraced seventh Earl Beauchamp, the story of Madresfield unfolds as part of a thousand years of English history.

ISBN 978-0-7531-8338-0 (hb)
ISBN 978-0-7531-8339-7 (pb)

ISIS publish a wide range of books in large print, from fiction to biography. Any suggestions for books you would like to see in large print or audio are always welcome. Please send to the Editorial Department at:

ISIS Publishing Limited
7 Centremead
Osney Mead
Oxford OX2 0ES

A full list of titles is available free of charge from:

Ulverscroft Large Print Books Limited

(UK)
The Green
Bradgate Road, Anstey
Leicester LE7 7FU
Tel: (0116) 236 4325

(Australia)
P.O. Box 314
St Leonards
NSW 1590
Tel: (02) 9436 2622

(USA)
P.O. Box 1230
West Seneca
N.Y. 14224-1230
Tel: (716) 674 4270

(Canada)
P.O. Box 80038
Burlington
Ontario L7L 6B1
Tel: (905) 637 8734

(New Zealand)
P.O. Box 456
Feilding
Tel: (06) 323 6828

Details of **ISIS** complete and unabridged audio books are also available from these offices. Alternatively, contact your local library for details of their collection of **ISIS** large print and unabridged audio books.